THE EUROPEAN HISTORY SERIES
SERIES EDITOR
KEITH EUBANK

THE ORIGINS OF WORLD WAR II

THIRD EDITION

KEITH EUBANK

QUEENS COLLEGE OF THE
CITY UNIVERSITY OF NEW YORK

HARLAN DAVIDSON, INC.
WHEELING, ILLINOIS 60090-6000

Visit us on the World Wide Web at www.harlandavidson.com

Library of Congress Cataloging-in-Publication Data

Eubank, Keith.
    The origins of World War II / Keith Eubank.— 3rd ed.
        p. cm. — (European history series)
    Includes bibliographical references and index.
    ISBN 0-88295-228-5 (alk. paper)
    1. World War, 1939–1945—Causes. 2. Europe—Politics and govern-
ment—1918–1945. 3. Germany—Foreign relations—1933–1945. 4.
National socialism. 5. Germany—Military Policy—History—20th
century. I. Title: Origins of World War 2. II. Title: Origins of World
War Two. III. Title. IV. European history series (Wheeling, Ill.)
    D741.E85 2004
    940.53'11—dc22

                                                            2003018351

Cover photo: The Reichstag cheering Hitler on March 13, 1938, at the
announcement of the union of Germany and Austria. *AP/Wide World*

Manufactured in the United States of America
06 05 04 03 1 2 3 4 MG

FOR DAVID AND ELLEN

CONTENTS

PREFACE

TO THE THIRD EDITION

Since the original writing of this book, new publications on the origins of World War II have made the study of this topic more complex. There still remains no simple answer to the question: "Why World War II?" Nevertheless, if we are to search for answers, it is necessary to examine the policies, the outlook, and the experience of the statesmen and politicians who wrestled with Adolf Hitler's demands, as well as the military, political and economic conditions of their nations. In addition, Hitler's responsibility for World War II has mounted as new evidence indicates that he craved the war he got in 1939 but failed to get in 1938. It is important also to study the policies of those who had to confront Hitler but did not understand his intentions and policies until it was too late. They preferred peace to another bloody conflict.

The aim of this book is to explain the origins of the world war that began in 1939 and ended in 1945 with 30,000,000 people dead and unbelievable devastation over much of the world. This book seeks answers to these questions. Why, after the ordeal of 1914–1918, did Western powers err in assessing the threat that loomed across the Rhine? Why was there so much reluctance on the part of Britain and France to confront the once defeated foe? Why had Germany been permitted to rearm? Why should Germany be allowed to occupy independent nations without a struggle?

Part of the answer, as I argue in these pages, can be attributed to the illusion that sufficient security measures were in place to maintain peace. The memories of the terrible destruction and loss of life during the years 1914–1918 seemed to make another world war unthinkable. But this illusion misled men and women into imagining that they were safe from another world conflict until they faced the necessity of choosing between surrender to an aggressor's demands or going to war again.

A major theme in this book is the role of appeasers in dealing with Hitler and in trying to avoid war. What was the purpose of a policy of appeasement? Why did the appeasers fail to perceive Hitler's intentions? Why were appeasers so reluctant to confront Hitler? Was there actually a purpose in appeasement? I have tried to show that appeasement was a policy with a history that had public approval. In analyzing appeasement, it is also necessary to examine the role of the British prime minister, Neville Chamberlain, who was not as foolish as some have imagined. As it turns out, Chamberlain does have his defenders. The Western democracies have been denounced for their failure to go to war against Germany before 1939. Such accusations fail to take into account the public mood and the lack of military preparedness on the part of France and Great Britain. It is important to realize that the Western leaders who had to make the decision for war or peace had grave doubts about the capabilities of their armed forces.

The myths that have emerged from the history of this era still flourish. They include the notion that Britain and France could have halted the German reoccupation of the Rhineland with ease had they only tried; that appeasement of Hitler was tantamount to cowardice on the part of Neville Chamberlain; and the fiction of Stalin's eagerness to save the world from Hitler.

I have sought to reassess Soviet policies in the light of more recent research which shows that they were never as altruistic as some have imagined. Some historians have condemned the French and British for failing to conclude an alliance with the Soviet Union in 1939; indeed, one can blame them for their shortsightedness in dealing with Stalin. At the same time, Moscow cannot be acquitted for its duplicity and opportunism in allowing Hitler to unleash his war which ultimately brought death and destruction to the Soviet Union.

During the Cold War, American politicians were influenced by the failure to confront Hitler in the years before 1939. Consequently alliances were created, plans developed and American troops stationed in Europe to prevent Soviet aggression.

When a crisis erupted over Soviet missiles in Cuba in 1962, sufficient American military forces were mobilized to force a resolution of the crisis. The United States government did not intend to pursue a policy of appeasement.

My intention in writing this book has been to present a concise explanation of the origins of this war in the light of recent research. I have tried to update this book and to provide new details about the events of this significant period of history. I hope that the bibliographical essay will aid readers in learning more about this subject.

These pages have profited from discussions with my students and colleagues when I was teaching at Queens Collage and at the Graduate Center of the City University of New York. I am grateful to the staff of the Benjamin Rosenthal Library of Queens College for seeking out-of-print books. More recently I am indebted to the staff of the Alderman Library at the University of Virginia for their kind and efficient aid. As always, I must take full responsibility for whatever errors and shortcomings are found in these pages.

Keith Eubank
Charlottesville, Virginia

1 / "PEACE," 1918-1933

NOVEMBER 11, 1918

When the slaughter across Europe ceased after 11:00 A.M. on November 11, 1918, and peace returned to the world, the extent of the devastation that lay about the exhausted armies was new to human history. After four years of war, the piles of stones, the battered chimneys, and the roofless houses were the only signs that people had once lived in peaceful towns and villages. The trenches where soldiers had burrowed, lived, fought, and died for a few yards of mud were mute evidence of the way of life that had destroyed the quiet countryside. The life and culture that were over had been Europe's greatest era. All that was left on the continent were the remnants of the four empires destroyed by the conflict. Over ten million people lay dead, and millions more had been wounded—but the cost in heartache and sorrow could not really be reckoned. What had begun with the murder of an Austrian archduke ended with millions of soldiers from many nations fighting across continents and oceans.

But the big losers were the countries of Europe. For Germany, the war had been a struggle for domination of world economy and trade, though the German leaders had led the German people to believe they were battling for survival against encirclement by Britain, Russia, and France. The vision of a German-dominated Europe that the German nationalists had grasped for vanished suddenly in the fall of 1918—but only after they had occupied Belgium, overrun northern France, and defeated Russia.

The German government sought peace then only because it feared utter destruction and because its leaders wished to save the army and keep the nation intact. Further fighting, they reasoned, could destroy the Fatherland without bringing victory

1

nearer. An armistice, on the other hand, could save Germany, giving the nation time to recuperate until it was better prepared to renew the war. The German civilians, however, were not prepared for the armistice. The High Command had not informed the nation of the plight of the armies, and the German countryside was almost completely untouched by war. Only a few villages in Alsace had been lost to the enemy—how, then, could the German people reconcile defeat? They had passed through three victorious wars of unification; and in this great war, they heard nothing but optimism from the front. Defeat was unheard of, and it would not be accepted.

The Entente powers were jubilant. The dancing, cheering throngs in Piccadilly and Times Square were delirious because their great efforts were over. The rejoicing was not so delirious in Paris because too many French families were in mourning for loved ones; to the French as well as to the other victorious nations, the possibility of another world war was unthinkable. One Austrian archduke had not been worth so many dead. World war must never come again; everything must be done to avoid it.

However, twenty-one years after, the unthinkable was to happen. This second world war of the twentieth century was never really inevitable: decisions, plans, mistakes, stupidities, fears, and all the unplanned and unexpected events in human life combined to bring it about. These events have their origins in the armistice that saved German unity and the German army, prevented Allied occupation, and thus left the German people unresigned to the collapse of their dreams. The terms of the armistice were drawn deliberately to ensure that Germany would be unable to renew the war. They required that German troops be withdrawn beyond the Rhine River while the Allied troops established bridgeheads on the right bank. Quantities of war materials and all of the submarine fleet were to be surrendered; sixteen capital ships were to be interned. Although Germany was to be unoccupied, the blockade would be continued.

Military occupation would have brought home to every German town the reality of defeat. But, saved by the armistice, the German army retired intact within the frontiers. Army units were welcomed back to their homeland with parades and cheering throngs, as though they were the victors instead of the vanquished. Because the army had not been routed and because German cities had escaped damage, army leaders were able to invent the myth of a "stab in the back"—the army had not been defeated on the battlefield but had been betrayed at home.

Under pressure from those in his government who wished to escape an onerous peace, Kaiser Wilhelm II had been forced to abdicate on November 9, 1918, in favor of a parliamentary monarchy. That same day, because of the outbreak of civil war and the fear of a Bolshevik-style uprising, the Social Democrat leader Philipp Scheidemann proclaimed a democratic republic. In one afternoon, Germany had adopted a form of government for which it was unprepared. Born in defeat, and shame, the Republic would be unable to avoid the stigma of the armistice, the "stab in the back," and the Treaty of Versailles, while the military leaders and the monarchy would be able to escape responsibility. The Weimar Republic—named for the city where its constitution was drafted—needed the loyalty of every German to survive, but never would all of the citizens back the strange new government with any enthusiasm. Too many people in high places were longing for the monarchy; and too many others were busy undermining the new government, even at its inception.

THE TREATY OF VERSAILLES

The delegates from twenty seven nations assembling in Paris in January 1919 faced a host of problems. The Peace Conference's foremost concern was to prevent German domination of Europe. There were other problems as well—many of them created by dissension among the victors themselves. Because of the enormous cost of the conflict, many were insisting that Germany pay the total cost of the war. New states had appeared, snarling over boundaries and populations; these had to be sorted out in some logical and equitable fashion. Italy was intent upon looting the remnants of the Austro-Hungarian Empire. Britain, Japan, and France insisted on dividing the German colonies among themselves. In the midst of all this, a scheme had to be devised to ensure peace in the future.

The Council of Four—Woodrow Wilson of the United States, Georges Clemenceau of France, David Lloyd George of Great

Britain, and Vittorio Orlando of Italy—dominated the Peace Conference. This quartet faced an enormous task—writing a peace treaty for Germany, working on treaties for the other defeated powers, restoring peace among the smaller European states, feeding the starving, establishing the League of Nations, and all the while continuing to govern their own nations. Not only did they lack the ability and temperament to accomplish their task, but each was so occupied with his own concerns that he failed to see the importance of the whole or the vital interests of the others. Wilson was chiefly interested in the League of Nations, insisting on inserting it in the treaty dealing with Germany. Orlando sought plunder for Italy, halting the conference with his demands, but Wilson forced his departure so they could get on with treaty writing. Lloyd George was concerned with insuring British naval supremacy, enlarging the empire, and reviving trade. Clemenceau was bent upon protecting France, which had been twice invaded by German armies in his lifetime.

The Treaty of Versailles was finally drafted by Wilson, Lloyd George, and Clemenceau, with limited help from the host of experts they had brought to Paris. Since 1919, the Treaty of Versailles has been severely criticized; but critics of the treaty have damned Clemenceau as the villain with Lloyd George as his accomplice, and have lauded Wilson as the White Knight who wanted to remake the world but who was thwarted by selfish European politicians. Actually, Wilson was more easily satisfied by the treaty than was Clemenceau, who, forced into compromises, warned his colleagues of the faults in the restrictions that they had placed—or had failed to place—on German might. It is true that Lloyd George achieved his aims in the treaty, but he alone attempted to improve it before Wilson left Paris. It was Wilson who was so in favor of the treaty as it was, consenting only to minor changes, as long as he had his League of Nations.

In May 1919, the treaty terms were presented to the German delegation, which was allowed to reply in writing but not to negotiate. Living in their dream world, unconscious of the hatred accumulated during the war, the delegation was shocked by the terms presented to them. But the Weimar government had little choice other than to accept the terms. A renewal of the war, the German generals advised, could bring an end to both the Ger-

German Territorial Losses in Central Europe, 1919

man army and German unity. In the Palace of Versailles on June 28, 1919, the German delegation signed the Treaty of Versailles—but it is now evident that the German nation never intended to abide by it.

The terms of the treaty tract been designed to render Germany helpless forever. The army was limited to 100,000 officers and soldiers serving a twelve-year term of enlistment; military conscription was forbidden; the General Staff was dissolved; military schools were restricted, the manufacture of arms and munitions was curtailed, and the export and import of them were forbidden; the navy was reduced and the air force outlawed. An Allied military control commission would supervise disarmament.

Germany was stripped of its colonies and was forced to cede territory to Denmark, Belgium, France, Czechoslovakia, and Poland. To give Poland an outlet to the Baltic Sea, East Prussia was detached by a strip of land that became known as the Polish Corridor, an area that included Danzig, which would be a free city under League of Nations administration. Not only would the Rhineland be occupied by Allied troops for fifteen years to ensure compliance with the terms of the treaty, but it would be permanently demilitarized—no German troops, no military weapons, no fortifications. The Saar area would be under the League of Nations for fifteen years after which a plebiscite would decide the final control.

The treaty also required that Germany pay for reparations, but because the Council of Four would not agree on the amount of reparations, it had to be determined after the peace conference by a special commission. To German patriots this seemed to be a "blank check" designed to ruin Germany forever; they were unwilling to conceive of any method whereby Germany would be able to pay reparations. Moreover, Germany did not want to pay reparations and was determined not to pay them.

Article 231, erroneously labeled "the war guilt clause," which introduced the reparations section of the Treaty of Versailles, and provided the legal basis for the reparations, was incomprehensible to the German population who had been told by the Imperial government that Germany had fought a defensive war. According to this clause, Germany accepted "the responsibility of Germany and her allies for causing all the loss and damage to which the Allied and Associated Governments and their nationals have been subjected as a consequence of the war imposed upon them by the aggression of Germany and her allies." The German people did not realize that this clause was also included in the peace treaties with Austria and Hungary; it never mentioned "war guilt." Allied leaders never imagined that Article 231 would be interpreted as a war guilt clause. The Allied leaders had never thought about writing such a clause. Moreover, the Allied leaders assumed that the Germans realized that they had lost the war and were responsible for the outbreak of the war. Nevertheless, the Weimar Republic assigned the task of refuting war guilt to a special office set up in the foreign ministry. This office subsidized books—suppressing some—

and hired journalists and historians to convince the world of German's innocence. Germany's resentment of the treaty of Versailles would help Adolf Hitler's rise to power.

Unemployed army officers, university professors, civil servants, and even clergymen swelled the chorus damning the treaty and the new republic that had accepted it. Rather conveniently they forgot that a precedent had been set for this kind of "war guilt" in the Treaty of Brest-Litovsk, March 3, 1918, when the Imperial German government had detached over one million square miles of Russian land (a deed remembered by Wilson). They ignored the heavy indemnity and the cession of Alsace-Lorraine that Bismarck had demanded of France in 1871. Most important, they failed to consider that, had Germany won in 1918, the defeated Allies would have paid heavier reparations and suffered a greater loss of land.

With the Treaty of Versailles, the Allies imagined they had found a means for preventing German domination of Europe; but the treaty was deceptive—its strength was an illusion. It was not harsh enough to render Germany impotent forever, but it was severe enough to provide German nationalists with a cause they could use to rally the nation against the treaty. British and American delegations had not hesitated to impose heavy obligations on Germany, but neither was willing to insist on a means to compel fulfillment of the terms. Both condemned French efforts to ensure German compliance. The French wanted the Treaty of Versailles to be a safeguard against future German aggression; but Wilson and Lloyd George assumed that Germany would willingly enforce the provisions, acting as its own policeman. Thanks to the Anglo-American objections, only the Rhineland would be occupied, and it was to be evacuated within fifteen years, providing Germany had fulfilled the Treaty of Versailles. Penalties for German violation of treaty terms were nonexistent. When the occupation of the Rhineland ended in 1930 ahead of schedule, and Allied troops withdrew, nothing remained within Germany to guarantee German observance of the treaty terms.

This is not to say that the Allies completely ignored the problem of policing German disarmament. It is simply that their policing never became effective. Except for the army of occupation in the Rhineland, Germany was unoccupied. However, the treaty set up the Allied Control Commission to insure German compliance, but its unarmed control officers encountered a well-organized attempt to frustrate their efforts. Using passive resistance, insults, and physical intimidation, the German army systematically blocked the Commission. In 1927, at German insistence, the Allied Control Commission was withdrawn, and its final report on German violations of the disarmament provisions of the Treaty of Versailles was ignored and suppressed.

The great industrial empire of Krupp diversified its operations, setting up satellite armament production centers in Sweden and in the Netherlands producing artillery, antiaircraft guns, and tanks. Tony Fokker, owner of the Fokker Aircraft Works, smuggled planes, parts, and equipment in trainloads to the Netherlands and soon began producing and selling planes.

The Reparations Commission set up by the treaty finally presented a bill to Germany and her former allies for $33,000,000,000 in gold. France needed reparations to pay its heavy reconstruction costs and the debts owed to Britain and the United States. Britain refused cancellation of debts owed by France unless the United States was willing to cancel British debts. But the United States was unwilling to cancel any debts whatsoever. In the words of President Calvin Coolidge, "They hired the money, didn't they?"

It is evident now that Germany never intended to pay reparations. The Weimar government requested a scaling down of payment and a new assessment of German ability to pay. The French rejected this flatly, arguing that, if neither London nor Washington considered French ability to pay, the yardstick should not be applied to Germany. An international conference to work out a new settlement might have been able to solve the muddle, but the United States refused to negotiate out of fear that the French and British might succeed in lowering their war debts. But the blame cannot be placed fully upon the United States nor upon the Allies in general. Certainly their failure to come to an agreement on reduction of reparations left Germany faced with the necessity of paying the full amount, but Germany was not so much weakened economically by the reparations as angered by them. What Germany ultimately paid in reparations proved to be far less than the total assessment.

Only one military attempt was made to enforce the reparations section of the treaty, and that attempt failed. After the Reparations Commission had declared that Germany had defaulted on coal quotas, French and Belgian troops were dispatched to occupy the Ruhr on January 11, 1923, and to seal the area off from the rest of Germany. Because of German destruction of French coal mines in 1918, France needed coal. German coal producers, however, were charging high prices for the coal shipped to France. In addition, France needed funds to finance heavy reconstruction in the war-devastated regions— an expense Germany had not incurred. The governments in Brussels and Paris were under the illusion that German workers could be compelled to labor for the victors. What they found was the contrary: workers in the Ruhr, urged on by the German government, struck and sabotaged their efforts. In an attempt to support the resistance, the German government increased the printing of money, with the result that the German economy suffered a disastrous inflation. The roots of the inflation can be found in the fiscal policy of the Imperial government, which financed the war through loans instead of taxes and used the printing press to pay for expenses, expecting the defeated Allies to pay for the war. Consequently the mark had already lost half its value by 1918. Where before the war the mark was valued at four to the dollar, by November 1923, it had been devalued to 4,000 million to the dollar. Many people had to resort to barter, while those who lived on fixed incomes were wiped out. Wages had such little buying power that the average workingman was hard put to purchase the barest necessities, while shrewd manipulators took advantage of the inflation to build up fortunes, and German industrialists paid off their indebtedness in worthless marks.

Eventually, the French and Belgian governments found occupation costs greater than they were able to collect in reparations. In addition, they were faced with the disapproval of the United States and British governments. Fearing the German financial problem would spread, they began an investigation into the problems of reparations. The result was the plan presented by the Dawes Commission, which proposed that reparations payments should be based on Germany's ability to pay, with that ability to be determined by an "index of prosperity." But the Dawes Plan did not stop there. It proposed international loans to help the German economy recover. France and Belgium accepted the plan in 1924 and withdrew their troops. Loans, chiefly from United States banks, poured into Germany, creating prosperity for the defeated country, although "victorious" Britain and France, who also owed war debts, were not permitted a similar advantage. With the United States loans, German industry was able to expand its war-making potential far beyond that of France and Britain.

Germany had managed to pull victory from defeat. After this, it would not be faced with French attempts to enforce the Versailles treaty alone. In addition, as if being rewarded for resistance, German industry was being heaped with financial aid from former enemies. Here, only five years after the close of war, the pattern was being set for what was to come. Germany was expressing dissatisfaction with the treaty it had "accepted," and the victors were making concessions that eventually would prove too liberal. They instituted the policy of appeasement that they later would curse bitterly.

In condemning French occupation of the Ruhr, the United States and Britain had pointed to the Treaty of Versailles, reasoning that this kind of action had not been provided for. But these would-be arbiters of international morality had little right to point. During the peace conference, Wilson and Lloyd George had signed separate mutual defense treaties with Clemenceau, guaranteeing aid to France in the event of German invasion. This guarantee was to last until the League of Nations had sufficient strength to impose peace, at which time France would have both the treaty and the League as bulwarks against German aggression. However, these agreements were not a part of Wilson's plans for Europe; they were simply temporary expedients he was willing to accept in order to circumvent Clemenceau's demands for detachment of the Rhineland. Neither he nor Lloyd George ever intended that the guarantee should become a permanent military alliance. The United States Senate only reinforced this intent when it refused even to consider the agreement after it had rejected the Treaty of Versailles. With Wilson's signature not worth the paper it was written on, Britain was not about to be bound by the guarantee.

Thus, deserted by its allies, France was left with only the League of Nations to protect its security, and that was cold comfort at best. France would be able to achieve security only by forcing Germany to adhere to the provisions of the Versailles treaty, but the devastated country could not accomplish alone a task that eventually would require the combined efforts of Britain, the United States, and Soviet Russia. Try as he might, Clemenceau would not be able to convince a distrustful Britain or an isolationist United States of the rightness of his cause. And certainly, France could not turn to Soviet Russia, which—enmeshed in its own internal problems and resentful of a peace settlement that excluded it—felt more sympathy for Germany than for France.

As a result, the treaty satisfied no one. Certainly, with the treaty rejected by the Senate, United States dissatisfaction was apparent. But the British critics had been outspoken against the treaty provisions even before the treaty was signed. They considered it a dictated peace, based on military power, and believed its "idealism" to be nothing more than hypocrisy. Self-determination, they pointed out, had been denied Germans in Austria and Czechoslovakia; the treaty spoke of territorial integrity, but Germany had been robbed of its own lands; and, most important to many of the critics, the enormous reparations would bar a return to prosperity. John Maynard Keynes denounced the reparations in one of the strongest assaults—and the most successful. In *The Economic Consequences of the Peace,* he claimed that the treaty was incompatible with overall European economic prosperity because it wrecked the German economy. If Europe were to recover, Germany had to recover; and this Germany could not do unless the treaty were revised. Keynes's arguments lent valuable assistance to the case for German appeasement, sustaining the plea that, because Germany had been so mistreated, it should be unilaterally allowed to revise the treaty.

During the 1920s and 1930s, it was in fashion to damn the treaty, but the criticisms were really unfair. After all, Germany had accepted the treaty, and Germany was unoccupied except for the Rhineland. And even that was to be evacuated before the expiration of the fifteen-year period set down in the treaty. The reparations Germany had to pay were high, but they were proportionately no heavier than those imposed on France in

1871, and France then had not received loans to speed its recovery. France had paid the reparations in order to be rid of an unwanted occupation army. There is no doubt that Germany could have paid the reparations had the nation been so inclined, and it actually would have been to its advantage. The industrial expansion resulting from endeavors to make payments would have given Germany economic hegemony in Europe.

Although the loss of its colonies wounded Germany's pride, there was no real damage. In fact, the German taxpayers should have rejoiced at getting rid of an unnecessary luxury. Once Germany had suffered defeat, the loss of Alsace-Lorraine was inevitable, but that was the only German territory given to France. Nor were the lands ceded to Belgium, Czechoslovakia, and Denmark crippling losses; and Poland had as much right to be an independent nation as Germany had. It is true that the separation of East Prussia from the rest of Germany caused by the creation of the Polish Corridor was not a natural geographical distinction, but it was not as vast a separation as that of Alaska from the United States. In terms of potential, the losses that Germany suffered were not as heavy as those imposed on Russia in the Treaty of Brest-Litovsk, when Germany had taken 54 percent of Russian industry and 34 percent of the Russian population.

Thus, the treaty of Versailles, contrary to the beliefs of early critics, left Germany's potential strength virtually untouched. In population, resources, and size, Germany was still the largest nation in Central Europe, except for the Soviet Union. And the war had not turned its soil into a wasteland as it had with French and Belgian land. Germany remained the industrial powerhouse of Europe despite the loss of iron ore from Lorraine and Saar coal. Although defeated, Germany suffered less damage in economic and human resources than the other major European belligerents. In spite of defeat, Germany remained the greatest economic power in Europe.

Germany was in an ideal position because the collapse of the Hapsburg empire, the defeat of Imperial Germany, and the Bolshevik victory in Russia created a power vacuum in eastern Europe. The only nation in a position to fill that vacuum was Germany. The fledgling nations stretching from the Baltic to the Mediterranean—with their oil, factories, farms, and natural resources—beckoned to the strongest bidder. Fashioned under the terms of the Treaty of Versailles, the German army was a long-term professional force, and it was the largest and most efficient in Central Europe. None of Germany's neighbors could afford so large a professional army—especially not France, whose forces were made up of conscripts led by antiquated generals.

Certainly the Treaty of Versailles deserved criticism, but the criticism it received was not the criticism it deserved. Even if the treaty had been amended in line with its criticisms, the events that were to take place in the ensuing two decades could not have been avoided.

The German people resented the Treaty of Versailles. As a result, their concerns aided Adolf Hitler's rise to power. The Treaty of Versailles offered him ammunition for his attacks on the Weimar Republic whose representatives had signed the treaty. Hitler's assault on the "Peace of Shame" struck a responsive chord with the audiences who came to hear his speeches. He succeeded in mobilizing resentment of the Treaty of Versailles for the sake of his cause—the overthrow of the Weimar Republic.

THE LEAGUE OF NATIONS

Imbedded in the Treaty of Versailles was the Covenant of the League of Nations, dear to the heart of Woodrow Wilson. It had been placed there at his insistence. According to the Covenant, the League of Nations guaranteed the territorial integrity and independence of all its members, but it did not stipulate how it would carry out its guarantee. It simply indicated that it would consider the act of any League member declaring war without completing the prescribed procedures for settling disputes as an act of war against the entire League of Nations. In the event of such an occurrence, League members were to impose economic and financial sanctions immediately. They were in no way obliged to make war on the aggressor or to contribute to armed forces that would enforce the League Covenant. The League Council could, however, "recommend" that its members contribute to such a force. This was complicated by the fact that, because all decisions of the Council, as well as the Assembly, had to be unanimous, swift action was absolutely impossible. In the event of Council failure to reach unanimous agreement on a means for ending a dispute, the League's members were to be free to take whatever action they deemed wise. This, of course, included the freedom to do nothing.

The League has been consistently blamed for the failure to prevent the outbreak of World War II. These charges generally have been unjust. The League of Nations was not intended as a military alliance, prepared to rush ships and troops to protect a nation from aggression. Those who drafted the Covenant believed that World War I could have been avoided if the great powers had possessed some means for delaying hostilities while they instituted negotiations to settle the disputes. They designed the League of Nations as a mechanism to delay the rush of nations into conflict, not to protect the victim from aggression by an alliance. There had been attempts to devise a military alliance, but these had been quashed by Wilson, who was a proponent of the theory that it was a confrontation between alliances that had started the war.

Thus, the League of Nations, like the Treaty of Versailles, created a false sense of security because many people imagined that it was poised, ready to move swiftly to punish the aggressor and enforce the peace; but, thanks to the conservatism of its creators and the power of nationalism, the League of Nations would not be equipped to handle the arduous labors that would be thrust upon it during its brief history. Idealists imagined that the League would be the supreme arbiter of international affairs, but the great powers who dominated the League would not permit it to handle matters vital to their national interests. They were willing to use the League when it suited them—when the disputes were minor affairs involving less powerful nations. But they were unwilling to give up a certain degree of their power in order to give the organization any real power of its own. Especially after the international crises broke out across Europe in the 1930s, the major powers were unwilling to make changes in the Covenant that would give the League sufficient strength to halt aggression.

The League experienced its first crisis involving a major power in 1923, when Benito Mussolini, the new Italian dictator, demanded indemnity for the Italian commission murdered while involved in delimiting the frontiers between Greece and Albania. Because the Greek government had rejected his exorbitant demands, Mussolini ordered the bombardment and occupation of Corfu. The League was at a loss for a way to resolve the situation. Deprived of the leadership of the great powers, particularly France and Great Britain, there was little the League could do. Britain would not press the Greek case for fear Italy would walk out of the League; and France could not be bothered with using the League against any country other than Germany. Because neither power would support the Greek appeal, the matter was shunted to a conference of ambassadors, which awarded Mussolini his indemnity, thereby enhancing the dictator's reputation for pugnacity and establishing a precedent for avoiding direct confrontation with Fascist aggression.

Perhaps the best illustration of the weakness purposely built into the League of Nations was the Manchurian crisis. In September 1931, alleging that Japanese interests were endangered, Japanese troops began a "police action" in Manchuria, resulting in the setting up of the puppet state of Manchukuo. In 1933, after the League of Nations adopted the report of the Lytton Commission condemning Japanese actions, Japan withdrew from the League. The recommendations of the Lytton Commission were notably fair and sensible—Manchuria should be administered by an autonomous government with ultimate sovereignty under China, but with international police to guarantee protection of Japanese interests. But, when Japan refused to abide by the solution, the League could do nothing more than refuse recognition to the stamps, money, and passports of the puppet state.

The only means available to enforce Japanese adherence to these recommendations were in the hands of the major powers, and they were only lukewarm in their support of the League action. While they did not want to sanction Japanese aggression, their own interests prevented them from actively supporting the League's resolution. Britain's new coalition government, though headed by Labor pacifist J. Ramsay MacDonald, was dominated by Tories, who preferred Japan to China because Japan was an old ally and would be more likely to defend British interests in Manchuria. Furthermore, the MacDonald government was too busy trying to avert national bankruptcy to be greatly concerned with events in the Far East. France could not be bothered because Japan was no threat to French borders; and the United States, still influenced by isolationism and not wishing to be over-committed outside its borders, barely managed a pronouncement of "non-recognition."

Though the Manchurian crisis was a second wound to the League of Nations, it was less a failure of the League than a failure of the countries responsible for the formation of the League. They had built the slow, inefficient, and cumbersome mechanism into the League Covenant, and they had failed to stand by the League in a moment of crisis. The only attempt to resolve this weakness occurred in 1932, when France attempted to have troops set aside in constant readiness at the disposal of the League; but, because this smacked of a superstate, Britain killed the proposal.

The weakness most often pointed out is that of the United States' failure to join the League. This has created the myth that American participation somehow would have strengthened the League and managed to stave off war. Actually, if the United States had taken an active role in the League, history would have been changed very little. United States participation would not have altered the basic weaknesses in the League's procedures. Even with the United States, these procedures would have remained to foster aggression. After all, a United States president had written these weaknesses into the League's Covenant. The only thing the United States could have done to maintain peace would have been to station American troops permanently in western Europe; but the average voter, congressman, and senator in the United States recoiled at such a thought. It would require a Pearl Harbor—an attack directly involving United States interests—for an American president to be able to commit American troops to the preservation of world peace.

FRENCH "SECURITY"

Until Hitler came to power; Europe was living in a fantasy world, wrapped up in the illusion that a conflict like the last could never be repeated because Germany had reformed and because the newly formed League would guard the peace. Only a madman would be willing to court another bloodbath to achieve power, and madmen could not become heads of governments. The only one of the Versailles powers to doubt the fantasy and to search for a greater security was France, which, finding security neither in the treaty nor in the League, immediately began to cast about for alliances.

France would have preferred the old alliance with Russia, but the Bolshevik revolution in Russia and the fear of a similar takeover at home forced France to turn to nations that were weak, disunited, and quarrelsome. The first steps in developing an alliance were an agreement with Belgium in 1920 and one with Poland in 1921. Both promised mutual aid in case of German aggression or German mobilization, or in case of any need to enforce the Versailles treaty. In 1924, France allied with Czechoslovakia to oppose restoration of the Habsburg and Hohenzollern monarchies. The French alliance system was completed by an agreement with Rumania in 1926 and one with Yugoslavia in 1927. France also sought to negotiate a pact with the British, but Britain was fearful of the old problem of competing alliances and the new problem of French domination of Europe.

Despite the external appearances, this latter fear had little basis for existence. The main cause for it was the French relationship to the countries of eastern Europe. Britain considered the Little Entente as being nothing more than a French puppet. However, this alliance—formed in 1920–1921 by Czechoslovakia, Yugoslavia, and Rumania as a protection against Hungary—was connected to France only insofar as France had its individual pacts with each of them. It was certainly nothing on the order of what Britain suspected it of being.

Furthermore, beneath the illusion of these alliances, there was little real strength. Each of these new nations was plagued with minority problems. Self-determination was proving easier to preach than to practice, and boundaries drawn up at the conference table were proving to be less distinct than the peacemakers believed.

In giving Posen and Polish Pomerania (the Polish Corridor) to Poland, the Versailles powers had given Poland a German minority as well. In 1921, after a short war with Russia, Poland gained territory from the Ukraine and White Russia that would reinstate the boundaries of 1772, but it also gave Poland a Russian minority consisting of $4^1/_2$ million Ukrainians and $1^1/_2$ million White Russians. As long as Poland had these minorities, good relations with Germany and Russia would be difficult if not impossible.

Poland was certainly not the ideal ally for an insecure France. To be of any assistance, Poland had to be strong; and, to gain strength, it was necessary to antagonize either Germany or Soviet Russia or both. As long as Germany suffered from the war and Russia labored to recover from its revolution, Poland could pretend to be a great power; but, because of a smaller population and poor industrial potential, Poland would not be able to achieve its dream before Germany and Russia would be able to reclaim their old power. Then, the minorities Poland had acquired would prove to be a disadvantage—indeed, they would be a threat to Polish independence. It is true the appearance was that of an advantage to France: Germany was faced with France on the west and Poland on the east. But France did not consider the possibility of a threat to Poland's own eastern border. Poland would never be able to engage all its forces against Germany as long as there was the threat of Russia to the east.

The other major ally of France—Czechoslovakia—was also strategically vulnerable. The new country was narrow and entirely cut off from the sea, surrounded by Germany, Austria, Hungary, Rumania, and Poland. And, like Poland, the Treaty of Versailles had given Czechoslovakia the problem of minorities with loyalties outside the prescribed borders. The Magyars in Slovakia beckoned to Hungary. The Sudeten Germans of Bohemia despised the Czechs and yearned to become part of Germany. To complicate this problem further, the fledgling nation snatched Teschen from Poland while the Poles had their backs turned trying to gain territory from Russia.

France's other allies—Rumania and Yugoslavia—had been similarly handicapped. The borders set down by the peacemakers for Rumania were disputed by Hungary, Bulgaria, and Russia, while those for Yugoslavia were challenged by Italy, Bulgaria, and Hungary. The peacemakers' attempts had been laudable;

had the boundary problems been as clearcut as they had envisioned, the result of their attempts might have been equally as laudable. As it was, they had created as many problems as they had solved.

By turning to these new nations—with their new problems—for alliances, France was creating more of a problem than it was solving. These allies had too many enemies—both foreign and domestic—to contribute much to the defense of France, but they all expected French troops to be ready to protect them. The system of alliances proved to be a misalliance, economically as well as militarily. Ideally, the French economy should have been a complement to the economies of its allies, but its problems and those of its allies were identical. France had agricultural surpluses, and so did its allies. What French allies needed were industrial goods, but French industry was barely adequate for French needs. As a result, the countries of eastern Europe turned to the only European power who could supply the industrial goods—Germany. It also proved to be Germany who would become the market for their surpluses in agricultural produce, oil, and raw materials.

To complete the insurance against German attack, France erected the Maginot Line. Stretching across northeastern France, it would protect Alsace-Lorraine with a series of interlocking concrete and steel fortresses with underground command posts, barracks, storerooms, kitchens, ammunition dumps, and powerhouses in each. An underground railroad would connect them. The planning behind this was indicative of the policy of the French General Staff, a policy based on the concept that a good defense is far better than a good offense. In the final test, the Maginot Line—like all the other guarantees—would not provide France with the security it needed.

GERMAN "GOOD FAITH"

With the Locarno Conference, the French security system suffered a deadly blow. Due primarily to the efforts of the German Foreign Minister, Gustav Stresemann, who feared another occupation of the Ruhr, Germany managed to remove a large part of the restrictions of the Versailles treaty. Stresemann, like other patriotic Germans, hated the treaty, but he saw that a continuation of open opposition would not restore Germany to its old position of power in Europe. He endeavored instead to subvert the treaty restrictions by evidencing German "good faith," an attitude intended to show that the new German government was as dedicated to the peace as were Germany's former enemies.

Stresemann's purpose was to rid Germany of the occupation troops in the Rhineland and to avoid a second Franco-Belgian occupation of the Ruhr. In January 1925, Stresemann queried the British government on the possibilities of the demilitarization of the Rhineland if Germany were willing to sign an agreement recognizing the present French-German boundaries. This would have been a German acknowledgment of French rights to Alsace-Lorraine, but the Allies were doubtful about the wisdom of making such an agreement. They were unwilling to withdraw from the Rhineland on schedule until they were certain that Germany had complied with the disarmament provisions of the Versailles treaty. Faced with distrust—if not opposition—from the military and the right-wing segments of his government, Stresemann hoped to be able to dissociate the disarmament question from any international negotiations. By succeeding in this, he achieved Germany's first major victory against the Versailles treaty.

The treaties signed at Locarno on October 16, 1925, said nothing about German disarmament. In effect these treaties gave much to Germany and required nothing of it. All the signators— Britain, France, Germany, Italy, and Belgium—guaranteed the frontiers between Germany and Belgium and between Germany and France as fixed by the Treaty of Versailles. The five powers also accepted and guaranteed the demilitarized zone of Germany. France and Germany, and Germany and Belgium promised not to attack or invade each other except in fulfillment of the obligations of the Covenant of the League of Nations or in self-defense. A violation of the guarantees by one of the signatories obligated the others to aid the aggrieved nation. Treaties of arbitration were signed, as well as treaties of mutual assistance between France and Czechoslovakia and France and Poland.

Through this agreement, Stresemann was sacrificing nothing that was German—he knew the Reichswehr was unprepared for an invasion of France. However, it was true that Germany was giving up rights in Alsace-Lorraine and guaranteeing the status quo of its western borders with France and Belgium; but the German government would not guarantee the eastern borders of Germany because it intended one day to regain territory that had been given to Poland.

Because France had been unable to obtain a guarantee of Germany's eastern border, the guarantee of the western border meant nothing. In effect, the treaties of Locarno meant that Germany was free to do as it wished in Poland and Czechoslovakia to whom France was committed; but, if France attempted to fulfill its commitments to these countries, it would be breaking the Locarno agreements unless Germany had first attacked France. France could no longer enforce the Treaty of Versailles. The only concession Stresemann had made in eastern Europe was to accept the arbitration treaties with Poland and Czechoslovakia, but he refused a guarantee for these treaties.

The road had been paved for the end of the occupation in the Rhineland. Germany was making a display of its good intentions. Because Germany had mended its ways, it was implied, the Allies should reciprocate by relaxing the Treaty of Versailles. Since Germany had guaranteed its frontiers with France and Belgium, it would be appropriate for the Allies to withdraw troops from the Rhineland. Stresemann and Germany were chipping away at the restrictions, to the effect that by 1930— five years ahead of the prescribed time—the Rhineland was no longer occupied.

The Allies had committed a grave mistake. Evacuation would not succeed in appeasing Germany for long. Had the occupation forces remained there until 1935, as the Versailles treaty had planned, the Nazi threat might have been averted. By that time the threat was so obvious that France and Britain probably would have kept their troops in the Rhineland until the danger passed. As it was, they gave in to a brief period of German good faith, thus losing their right to intervene when the danger had returned. Having thrown away their strategic advantage, the Allies received no thanks from Germany. Instead, they were met with more demands for concessions.

Again, the mistake had been made despite French protests. Aside from Germany, the country most pleased with the results of the Locarno Conference was Britain, which accepted the pledges precisely because they were worthless. If the treaties of Locarno had committed Britain to a war in eastern Europe or if they had required a military alliance in western Europe, Britain would not have agreed to them. The vagueness of five nations allied against "aggression," but not against an aggressor; delighted the British government. Besides the promises in eastern Europe, France had wanted a promise of immediate military aid in ease of aggression; but Britain would allow no such thing.

Germany played upon the lack of commitment among the Allies. By 1926, it had gained admission to the League of Nations; and, by 1927, with Stresemann's guidance, it managed to achieve the end of the Allied Control Commission and to have the Commission's final report suppressed. German "good faith" was achieving the desired results. By creating the illusion of peace while secretly rebuilding its armed forces, Germany was on the way toward its goal of tearing up the Versailles treaty.

To complete the illusion of peace, negotiations were instituted in 1928 that led to the Kellogg-Briand Pact, renouncing war as a means for resolving disputes and pledging peaceful settlement of all agreements. Starting as a Franco-American agreement, this pact that was to outlaw war for all time would eventually be signed by sixty-five nations, including the Soviet Union. Who could find fault with so noble a principle? The signing and ratification by so many nations bore witness to the power of the illusion that another world war was impossible. The problem with this peace effort—as with others in this period—was that the peacemakers' blind optimism failed to consider a means for enforcing the peace in case one of the members broke the faith, as indeed one would do.

ECONOMIC CRISIS

The optimism of the peace—both in Europe and in the United States—was marred at this time by economic failures. The American stock market crash in 1929 was an indication of the dangers ahead for Europe. Immediately, it had the effect of a forced recall of loans made to Austria and Germany. It had been these loans, effected under the Dawes Plan, that had made possible the resurgence of the German economy. Now their withdrawal had the opposite effect. In 1930, the money market of Central Europe was gradually tightened, forcing industry to restrict production. In May 1931, the collapse of the Kreditanstalt, the largest Austrian bank, set off a series of bank failures throughout Central Europe. The resulting fall in production and prices brought widespread unemployment, with all of Europe suffering.

Ignorant of the subtleties of economics, the conservative European financiers argued that the depression could be ended only by balancing budgets, cutting government expenditures, and lowering taxes—all of which they proceeded to do, thereby making things worse. Requests from the military for armaments consistently encountered the argument that manufacturing useless weapons would call for increased taxes, and increasing taxes would prolong the depression. In Britain during these years, it became standard procedure to lower military budgets annually. After all, the government had adopted the rule that no major war was expected for ten years. However, whether from economic foresight or from military persistence, Germany managed to find the means to increase military expenditures, thereby rebuilding the army and keeping some people employed.

The unemployed were crying out for action from their various governments, thus lending encouragement to economic nationalism and frequently resulting in leaders adopting irresponsible measures that were harmful to other nations. While President Franklin D. Roosevelt's domestic program had its benefits, his foreign policy had disastrous results. In 1933, the major powers met in London to attempt to reach an agreement on stabilizing international currency exchange. But Roosevelt personally destroyed their hopes by refusing to accept any agreement they might make and by insisting on maintaining his isolationist monetary policy. This is not to say that, if he had agreed to negotiate, Europe's economic problems would have been solved, but it would have left the door open for some sort of economic cooperation on an international level. By being unwilling to face this struggle, Roosevelt unknowingly was increasing the possibilities for a greater struggle later on. Left to their own devices, the countries of Europe grasped at whatever straws looked promising.

In Germany, the more than six million unemployed grasped for any promise of an active program to replace the confusion of the Weimar Republic. This proved to be a boon to the rising Adolf Hitler. The political fortunes of this man, who otherwise might have been nothing more than a troublesome rabble-rouser, thrived on the depression. For a country accustomed to strong leadership, the confusion of the more moderate leaders seemed fearful. The German people looked Left and Right, seeking strength in extremes. When membership in the Communist party rose, many a good German citizen saw in Hitler the only bulwark against bolshevism. The disappointment, uncertainty, and fear of the time left the German people open for the endeavors of a demagogue.

2 / THE UNEASY PEACE,

1933–1935

ADOLF HITLER

Adolf Hitler, the shiftless son of an Austrian customs official, was born on April 20, 1889, in Braunau-am-Inn, near the Bavarian frontier. A lazy student whose grades were generally either poor or failing, he never completed his schooling. Although he had twice failed to gain admittance to the Vienna Art Academy, he was totally unprepared for any trade or profession. Incapable of holding a steady job, he existed on an allowance from his father's estate, enhanced by cheating his sister and his mother out of their share. Despite his failure to gain entrance to the Art Academy, he continued to live in Vienna, disdaining regular work. Eventually, he was reduced to living in public shelters and men's hostels. Proclaiming himself an artist, he painted picture postcards which a friend sold for him. At the same time, through his reading and his arguments, he began to fashion his political philosophy that was founded upon antisemitism, German nationalism, and his version of socialism. All things considered, he was a most unlikely candidate for the savior of Germany.

To evade his military service in the Austrian army, Hitler moved to Munich in 1913, but when this draft dodger was found, he was rejected as unfit for military service. At the outbreak of World War I, however, Hitler enlisted in the Bavarian army. Army life not only supplied him with a financial income and comradeship, but it also presented him with what he considered a profound experience. War, he found, was not hideous, but heroic and glorious; it gave purpose and meaning to his life. Hitler's regiment, thrown into the first battle of Ypres, saw heavy action throughout the war. Serving as a dispatch runner, a dangerous job, Hitler was wounded, gassed, promoted to lance corporal, and twice decorated with the Iron Cross. After the war, he was not likely to let this moment of glory pass.

Following the armistice, Hitler returned to Munich and continued to serve in the army as a political agent. Among his duties was that of indoctrinating soldiers with nationalistic, anti-communist ideals and keeping track of right-wing political parties. Following orders, on September 12, 1919, Hitler attended a meeting in a Munich beer hall of a small right-wing party, the German Workers' Party. While involved in his investigation, he became interested in the activities of this little group and accepted their invitation to join. It was not long before he controlled the organization. Because there were only about forty members, he had no trouble in dominating the party and exploiting it for his own personal power. The new leader built the membership, broadened the party's program, and changed its name to the National Socialist German Workers' Party, soon to become known to history as the Nazis.

It was only after he had begun serving the party that Hitler fully developed his talents as a demagogue. He spoke on Munich street corners, from the platforms of great auditoriums, and in smoke-filled Munich beer halls, denouncing the Versailles treaty, the Bolsheviks, and the Jews as the reasons for Germany's problems. For him, the spoken word was becoming a weapon that he could use with masterly skill to bring the German masses under his spell.

The German people did not want to hear dull statistics or long-winded political platitudes. They wanted to be absolved from the guilt of 1918 and from the disgrace of the Versailles treaty. They wanted someone to soothe their fears of inflation and depression. When Hitler stepped on the platform in a great auditorium, he was able to grasp this and give them what they wanted—impassioned oratory that would obliterate all common sense and give them something they could believe in so strongly that they would be willing to die for it. He gave them the image of a dynamic, authoritarian leader who would rescue Germany from disgrace and return it to a position of dominance in Europe.

Although Hitler must personally bear the greatest burden of guilt for World War II, he could never have come to power had World War I not made German values so unnatural. Certainly, he could never have attained power under the Hohenzollerns. The German system of values was inverted still further by an exaggerated fear that the Bolshevik revolution in Russia might be repeated in Germany The Nazis pointed to the Communist minority—small and ineffective, but Communist nevertheless—that had managed to find its way into the Reichstag. They provided Hitler with another target to add to his favorite—the Weimar Republic.

The occupation of the Ruhr in 1923 caused turmoil in Germany. By summer, the German economy was in a state of collapse. Inflation was rampant. There were rumors and plots for a march on Berlin to overthrow the republic and establish a right-wing government. In conservative Bavaria, on November 8, 1923, in a meeting in a Munich beer hall, Hitler proclaimed a revolution and a new Reich government. He sent some of his followers to seize important points in the city. They were generally unsuccessful. In a desperate effort, the next morning Hitler led his followers in a march through Munich hoping to arouse the population to overthrow the government. Eventually the demonstrators encountered a police cordon. Shots were fired and four policemen and fourteen demonstrators were killed. The man marching beside Hitler was killed. Hitler escaped with only a dislocated shoulder. His supporters deserted him, and the Beer Hall *Putsch* was a failure.

The future Fuehrer was tried and received a five-year sentence, but he was pardoned after serving only one year. In Landsberg prison, Hitler served his sentence in a large pleasant room with a lovely view of the countryside. His tastefully furnished room was daily thronged with so many visitors that eventually they had to be limited.

Hitler learned two lessons from his from his failure: he could not seize power through violence and he needed the support of the army. Despite the failure of the Beer Hall *Putsch*, Hitler gained a national reputation that he could build upon. To capitalize on this reputation, Ritler began writing a book while in prison. The result—*Mein Kampf* (My Battle)—failed in its goal;

instead of attracting further attention, the book would not become popular until after Hitler had achieved national prominence.

In 1933 it sold over a million and a half copies. Some have considered *Mein Kampf* to be a carefully contrived program for world conquest, but the book was never intended as anything of the sort. In fact, Hitler's publisher had hoped for a personal record of the struggles of Hitler and his little band of Nazis. What Hitler gave him was a badly written, rambling collection of threats, denunciations, and cries for vengeance from a minor German politician who seemed to have little chance of obtaining high political office.

What Hitler presented to his receptive audience, both in his book and in his speeches, was not a plan for conquest but a set of goals for Germany. *Lebensraum,* or "living space," was needed if Germany was to have sufficient population, food, and natural resources to dominate Europe. This required control of territory in Central Europe and in Russia as well as the union of the German peoples, who were now divided among several countries. The need for the destruction of France—and later of England—came from their existence as barriers to German domination of Europe. Certainly, in the early years, Hitler did not have a master plan to conquer the world through world war.

Rather, Hitler was an opportunist, ready to seize any chance to achieve his goals. In accomplishing what he did, he was aided by his patience and his masterful sense of timing. In the power vacuum of Central Europe, Hitler found his greatest opportunity, one had been created for him by the defects in the peace settlement. Between Germany and Russia lay a collection of small states that were weak, quarrelsome, deficient in population and industry; and none of them had an army approximating that permitted Germany by the treaty. To cap it off, each of these countries had minority problems that Hitler could exploit.

It is rare that an opportunist has had the wealth of opportunities that were presented to Hitler. In the beginning, when he first started to take control of the Nazi organization and build its membership, he saw confused men who had fought in the trenches, disgusted with the defeat, despairing at economic difficulties, and searching for someone—anyone—to blame for the misfortunes they were unable to understand. A better opportunity could not have been set up for a right-wing demagogue. Even something as unlikely as the advent of the airplane was an opportunity just waiting for the rising politician. By using the airplane in conducting his political campaigns, he was able to make himself known in every important German city and town, taking his carefully staged rallies to the masses. Though he lost the presidential election of 1932, he managed through his whirlwind campaign to make himself and his ideas known all over Germany.

Possibly the strangest of his opportunities came to him in the form of Joseph Stalin. Whether it was because he was still new to international affairs or because he was misinformed, it is hard to say; but whatever the reason, the usually clever Stalin erred in his assessment of nazism as fully as did the bourgeois capitalist politicians. What Stalin saw in Germany in 1930 was a parliamentary government headed for collapse because neither a single party nor a coalition could achieve a majority. Because he considered the Social Democrats—the leading party in the foundation of the Weimar Republic—to be seducing German workers from the Marxist faith, he was easily misled in appraising the Nazis. Stalin saw them as the natural Fascist prelude to the inevitable Communist revolution, and he allowed German Communists to cooperate with the Fascists in smashing the Social Democrats and disrupting the Weimar Republic. Had Hitler been an ordinary politician, Stalin's plans might have succeeded; but Stalin had not reckoned with an inspired demagogue.

The western political leaders, however, were so befuddled at being faced with a man unlike anyone they had ever had to deal with that they hurried to order the objects of Hitler's wrath to surrender lest he launch a war. This former inhabitant of the Vienna gutters and the Munich slums, who had survived by learning the intricacies of hitting below the belt and stabbing in the back, had the advantage over the people who knew only the standards of Whitehall and the Quai d'Orsay.

Hitler was seldom troubled by the unfavorable opinions of experts and professional diplomats, and he did not shrink from policies frightening to those with traditional attitudes on international affairs. Knowing that average men and women recoiled at the thought of a repetition of the kind of slaughter that occurred at Verdun, Hitler threatened it to frighten his opponents into concessions. After the fact, some historians have argued that Hitler's threats were bluffs, but the events of September 1939 prove that he was quite prepared to carry out his threats. Perhaps it was because they never had the responsibility for calling a bluff with empty hands that these historians can attribute a bluff to Hitler in 1938.[1]

The people helping Hitler made up one of the most curious phenomena of the time. The curiosity is not how few opposed Hitler but how many served him gladly—intelligent men and women who cheered his speeches, obeyed his laws, and ultimately died for him in the Russian snows and the Berlin rubble. Few dared question the goals that Hitler revealed in his statements to German officials, in his speeches to the nation, and in *Mein Kampf.* Who knows how many Germans understood his goals fully, but did not flinch from carrying out his orders despite the cost? Professional diplomats, generals and admirals, industrialists, civil servants—all carried out their duties as loyal German citizens, with only an occasional complaint sotto voce.

Perhaps each of them, caught up in his own immediate situation, believed he was responding as well as he could. Certainly, there were members of the High Command—some of the older officers—who were disgusted by Hitler's tactics, but who hoped they could tame him in order to use his Nazi party to provide mass support for the army's expansion efforts. These were officers who foolishly believed that Hitler's goals coincided with theirs, the only difference being that he craved them more speedily. The only goal for them was the rebuilding of the army and thereby regaining the German stronghold in Europe. If Hitler could help them to achieve this end, they would make allowances for any minor disagreements they might have.

Since Hitler had been proclaiming his purposes while welding Germany into a mighty war machine, why was there no one who would halt him before he conquered most of Europe? The answer is that there was no one who wanted to stop him. He seemed either to be an unpleasant nightmare that would swiftly vanish if everyone talked loudly enough about collective security or to be a politician who delivered bombastic speeches solely for German consumption. Hitler could never have been checked without a war ultimately involving most of Europe. At that price, no one cared to stop him. Until Hitler actually started the war, every nation shrank from checking him for fear that they might bring on a conflagration like the last.

REARMAMENT AND DISARMAMENT

When Hitler became chancellor on January 30, 1933, he could not immediately launch an aggressive foreign policy, but had to bide his time, consolidate his regime, and rearm the nation. Although, despite the provisions of the Versailles treaty, limited rearmament had been going on secretly during the Weimar period, the armed forces were still inadequate for the ambitions of the new chancellor. He did not conceal his goals from those whose support he needed. At a private dinner on February 3, 1933, he informed prominent members of the High Command that if Germany were to regain its position of power in Europe, the armed forces would have to be rebuilt by universal military conscription. Once the armed forces regained their strength, Germany would be able to acquire the much needed *Lebensraum* in eastern Europe.

Of course, the armed forces Hitler inherited could not be considered puny by any standards. In the dark days immediately following World War I, a brilliant staff officer, Hans von Seeckt, managed to keep the German army intact, thus easing Hitler's labors by laying the foundations for the mighty Wehrmacht. During the war, this aristocratic Prussian officer had helped achieve the breakthrough on the Russian front. After the war, in 1920, when he was appointed chief of the Army Command, he was given greater authority than any previous military commander in German history. Seeckt immediately set out to rebuild the army within the limitations of the Versailles treaty, making preparations for further expansion once Germany was free of the treaty.

Because of his negative attitude toward the Weimar Republic, Seeckt had created his army as a state within a state, an enemy of the Republic but a servant of "Germany." As such, there were subtle ways the army was able to get around the treaty provisions.

Although the treaty had abolished military training schools, Seeckt managed to turn the army into one great school, not only training soldiers but also encouraging the officers to formulate new tactical doctrines, study foreign military thought, and produce studies on the uses of new weapons. To avoid the restrictions the treaty placed on armaments, Seeckt had established secret arms depots that could be moved whenever necessary to escape detection by the Allied Control Commission. He had joined with the Krupp munitions firm to develop plans for new kinds of artillery, armor plating, anti-aircraft guns, and tanks. Through secret arrangements with the Soviet government, he had managed to establish a pilot training school, a tank school, an aircraft factory, a poison gas factory, and a shell factory all on Russian soil. The General Staff, strictly forbidden by the treaty, managed to continue functioning by camouflaging its activities in government ministries, civilian offices, and the Truppenamt (troop office) of the army.

If it had not been for the efforts of Seeckt, Hitler's plans probably would have taken much longer than they did. As it was, Hitler's eagerness to build the army could not be restrained. On February 8, only nine days after Hitler had taken over as chancellor, his cabinet learned that he was negotiating with the Allied powers to nullify the armaments section of the Versailles treaty to obtain equality in armaments for Germany. But what Hitler was aiming at was full rearmament—superiority, not equality. Once Germany possessed sufficient weapons and trained troops to alter the balance of power in Europe, Hitler could ignore the Versailles treaty entirely. He informed the cabinet that "for the next four/five years the main principle must be: everything for the armed forces. Germany's position in the World was decisively conditioned upon the position of the German armed forces."[2]

The first obstacle Hitler faced in achieving this end was the Geneva Disarmament Conference, which had opened in February of the previous year after many years of debate, wrangling, and planning. In the year preceding Hitler's ascendancy, Germany's representatives had been, first, Chancellor Heinrich Bruening himself and, later, Chancellor Franz von Papen's emissary, General Werner von Blomberg. Nevertheless, Hitler made himself felt at the conference. Bruening, soon to fall from power but desperately trying to hold on to his office, gave in to the Nazi pressure to take a hard line at the conference by insisting that all nations join Germany in "disarmament." But Hitler did not have to pressure Blomberg, who would later be his Minister of Defense and who was already enjoying the future Fuehrer's confidence.

The "equality" in armaments sought by Germany at the conference was aimed not so much at achieving disarmament by the other countries as at acquiring recognition by these countries of Germany's equal position among nations. After all, it was a full member of the League of Nations: should it have resitictions placed on it that were not placed on other nations?

In September 1932, because the German claim had not been recognized in principle, the German delegation withdrew from the conference. The major powers had second thoughts and quickly moved to appease the Germans. On December 11, they promised Germany "equality of rights in a system which would provide security for all nations."

When the German delegation rejoined the conference in February 1933, it was in a full sense Hitler's delegation; once gratified in its demands, it was ready to push on for more.

The promise of equality of armaments between France and Germany—resricting the land armies to the same size—would not satisfy Hitler. Nor was he satisfied with the five-year period for disarmament prescribed by British Prime Minister Ramsay MacDonald's plan. Hitler pretended to want worldwide disarmament, effected in less time. On May 17, 1933, he warned the conference that, if other nations did not disarm, Germany would insist on rebuilding its army to equal size. Part of his reason for this move was to provoke France—which would be relegated to an army of 200,000 with an overseas force of 200,000—to strenuous objection, thereby wrecking the conference altogether.

When the conference resumed in the fall of 1933 after a brief recess, the French presented a new plan that called for a four-year freeze on armaments while disarmament supervision was tested. If the supervision were successful, then all the powers would disarm in the following four years, making disarmament take up an eight-year period in total. Neither the inspection nor the eight years was palatable to Hitler. When Britain, the United States, and Italy supported the French plan, Hitler was backed into a corner. The supervision of the disarmament would uncover German violations of the Versailles treaty, and the eight-year period could not be adjusted to German industrial needs.

On October 14, Hitler announced German withdrawal from the Disarmament Conference and from the League of Nations as well, contending that equality of rights had been withheld from the German people. At the same time he dissolved the Reichstag, ordering a new election and announcing a plebiscite on the issue of withdrawal from the League of Nations as a vote of confidence in his actions. Of those Germans entitled to vote, 96 percent went to the polls, and 95 percent voted their approval of Hitler's policy.

He challenged the major powers by informing them baldly that German national interests were not subject to internationial conferences. Britain, France, and Italy continued to try to resolve the difficulties with Germany, but to no avail. There was no way the Treaty of Versailles could be invoked against Hitler.

In December, a secret conference of military leaders in Berlin drafted plans for a threefold increase in the size of the army. A four-year program commencing April 1, 1934, would create a 300,000 man, twenty-one division army by 1938. The goal of the plan was a field army that would be capable of fighting a defensive war on several fronts with good prospects for victory. Such a force would be a clear breach of the Versailles treaty.

THE FOUR-POWER PACT

An attempt to deal with other aspects of the treaty revision also failed. In March 1933, Mussolini presented a plan for a European directorate to be composed of Italy, Germany, France, and Great Britain. The directorate would be responsible for maintaining the peace and for making necessary revisions in peace treaties. Mussolini's proposition belied his hopes for Italy. It favored the four powers to the disadvantage of the countries of eastern Europe. He thought that the pact would give him a free hand in Austria and Yugoslavia, and thus help to establish Italy permanently as a great power. By freeing Germany from the fetters of the Treaty of Versailles and giving it a position of equal power, Mussolini hoped to reassure himself that Hitler had no aggressive intentions toward Italy.

When the pact was finally signed in July, it had been watered down by French objections to far less than Mussolini had hoped. The pact never had a chance to be effected because, before the countries involved had a chance to ratify it, Germany withdrew from the League of Nations and the Disarmament Conference. The only purpose it served finally was to turn Poland against France, thereby giving Hitler a new victory. Hurt by French failure to respond to its demands for equal position among the nations of Europe and alarmed by the German departure from the League of Nations, Poland turned to Hitler for a pact that would, in effect, nullify its earlier pact with France. On January 26, 1934, Poland promised that agreements with a third party (France) would not hinder peaceful relations with Germany; and both nations pledged to use peaceful means to reach a settlement if disputes arose. The pact would run until 1944. Hitler had achieved his first significant diplomatic victory.

THE DOLLFUSS AFFAIR

Hitler's luck failed him in his next endeavor outside German territory. Austria, under the leadership of Chancellor Engelbert Dollfuss, was a primary target for Hitler. German *Anschluss* (union) was necessary for German *Lebensraum*. Though it is probably true that Hitler had no direct involvement in the events in Austria in July of 1934, he must be considered indirectly responsible. He had expressed in *Mein Kampf* the need for *Anschluss*, and his radio had been broadcasting calls to Austria to rejoin Germany, by any means necessary, even murder.

The person standing in the way of achieving these goals, and thus the person Hitler hoped to see murdered, was Chancellor Dollfuss, a Christian Socialist who refused to accept all of the Nazis' demands. Never a lover of democracy, Dollfuss in March 1933 suspended Parliament because of a deadlock with the Social Democrats; ultimately, in May 1934, he banned political parties and promulgated a new authoritarian constitution. But urged on from Germany, Austrian Nazis demanded complete surrender to their demands, which would have given them control of the government. At the same time, they sabotaged Dollfuss's efforts to negotiate an agreement with them by initiating a campaign of terror.

Upset with Dollfuss and influenced by German radio propaganda, a small group of conspirators dressed in Austrian army uniforms took control of the Vienna chancellery on July 25, 1934, assassinating Dollfuss and announcing his resignation over the government radio. The coup was poorly organized and did not last long before the goverment was able to resume control. Presumably, the conspirators expected Hitler to come to their assistance, but circumstances were such that this was impossible. The Austrian people did not support the Nazis, while the Austrian army helped suppress the attempted coup.

When Hitler first received news of the coup, he was elated, and he followed carefully the developments occurring in Vienna. Although he had his Austrian Legion poised along the Austrian border, Hitler hesitated to enter the country unless the coup was overwhelmingly successful. When news reached him that Italian troops had been rushed to the Brenner Pass to halt any German invasion, he knew he could take no action. Actually, no troops had been dispatched; those at the Brenner Pass were there simply on maneuvers. However, their presence had the effect of an Italian move. Immediately, Hitlers radio changed its tune from congratulating the Austrian revolutionaries to consoling the Austrian government.

Fearful of being involved with the unsuccessful conspirators, Hitler publicly condemned their actions. When he was further embarassed by the fact that some German Nazis were involved in the affair, he tried to save face by ordering them to cease meddling in extra-national concerns. Though the failure of the Austrian coup did not have an effect on Hitler's goals, it forced him to alter his tactics somewhat, making him wait until he had a mighty German army at his command.

GERMANY'S MILITARY RENAISSANCE

After his success with Poland, Hitler again stated his policy to a selected audience of army and S.A.[3] leaders, informing them on February 28, 1934, that Germany would be faced with "frightful destruction" unless it could find sufficient living space for its people. The living space he suggested was to be found to the east, but, because the western European powers would be certain to oppose him, he proposed to strike at the west first and then turn east. This effort, however, would require a massive, well-trained army. He had two choices for achieving this: he could build upon the well-structured Reischswehr or he could turn to the S.A. brawlers. Their leader, the notorious Ernst Roehm, wanted a "second revolution" with the S.A. leadership assuming command and the S.A. absorbing the Reichswehr. Such a fate the generals would not tolerate. But Hitler had learned a lesson from the failed Munich Beer Hall *Putsch*: avoid an open conflict with the regular army. Moreover, for his rearmament program to suceeed, he needed the expertise of the army leadership. The S.A. and its ambitious leaders would have to be dispensable. He proved their dispensability on June 30 by liquidating the S.A. leadership.

When President Paul von Hindenberg died on August 2, 1934, the army repaid Hitler for purging the S.A. hierarchy by allowing Hitler to combine the offices of president and Reich chancellor in the new office of Fuehrer and Reich chancellor. To seal the bargain, officers and soldiers took a personal oath of allegiance to Hitler as the "Fuehrer of the German Reich and people."

Expansion of the armed forces required bringing some activities out into the open. The launching of warships and the testing of fighter planes could not be hidden for long. In addition, if Hitler intended to intimidate or to threaten European nations, he required a visible military force. But Hitler restrained himself from denouncing the armament restrictions on Germany until after the Saar plebiscite on January 13, 1935. This was the date set by the Treaty of Versailles for self-determination of the Saarlanders. The French and British had hoped that the removal of this grievance would pacify the Germans. Instead, the German government was freed of restraint. Rather than feeling grateful, Hitler regarded the Saar plebiscite as proof of the growing power of Nazi Germany. After the Saarlanders had voted solidly in favor of returning to Germany, Hitler could begin to unveil German military power.

On March 9, 1935, the German government announced the existence of the German air force. Then, when the French government doubled the term of military service and lowered the age of enlistment to compensate for a lower birth rate in the years from 1914 to 1918, Hitler had an excuse for his next action, promised to his generals on February 3, 1933, and postponed only because of international conditions. On March 16, he announced conscription and a thirty-six division army. His announcement was not a sudden, personal decision but reflected long-term, secret planning by staff officers. The German people hailed this military rebirth with great joy. Once more, Hitler's popularity soared. Germany's wartime enemies, fearful of provoking another world war for which they were unprepared, consequently did nothing to stop him. Short of war, little could have been done.

When Sir John Simon, the British foreign secretary, and Anthony Eden visited Germany later that month, they protested mildly about the air force and suggested joint efforts at coming to some sort of disarmament agreement. But Hitler taunted his guests with the comment—later proved to be a lie—that the German air force had already achieved parity with the R.A.F., and that he would in no way be interested in giving up that position.

Both Britain and France issued statements of protest and began to take steps toward rearmament, but they were reluctant efforts in comparison to those of Germany. As usual, the other European powers turned to conferences and joint statements to reassure themselves that peace would continue, blindly believing that talk would make action unnecessary. In April, Pierre Laval, the new French premier, met with MacDonald and Mussolini in Stresa, Italy, where they solemnly announced opposition to "any unilateral repudiation of treaties which may endanger the peace of Europe." To further console themselves, they reaffirmed their obligations as outlined by the treaty of Locarno. The Stresa Front, as this united action was labeled, was widely heralded as a barrier to Hitler.

But this action would prove insufficient to deter the massive moves of the German Fuehrer. Hitler was building a weaponry that would enable Germany to win by *Blitzkrieg*—surprise attack, swift invasion, exploitation of the confusion, and quick victory. As long as he had such superiority in weapons, Hitler did not need a superiority in numbers of troops. He preferred this kind of warfare because it achieved his goal swiftly—i.e., restoring Germany to world power—with only a portion of the economy geared to war. Total rearmament—troops as well as weapons— would require a complete overhaul of the economy, thereby frightening the country and shaking its faith in the Fuehrer. He hoped to avoid world war, because world war would mean austerity for the German people, and he knew that the German people wanted prosperity.

Just as a weapons superiority was suited to the German economy, the new German army and the German geographical location were suited to blitzkrieg warfare. Surrounded by weak nations too often interested only in quarreling with each other, Germany could move in lightning attacks and acquire territories one by one without giving the other major powers time to object. And, as long as Germany did not have a massive army, the major powers would not have reason to fear it.

Opposition to this military policy did develop later. Some army officers were disturbed that, if the conflict burgeoned into a world war of the proportions of 1914–1918, the German army would not be prepared. (Essentially, this is why Hitler would finally be defeated.) Hitler, however, opposed the long-range economic planning that this required. Long-range economic planning and rearmament for world war could create powerful vested interests that could oppose his dictatorship. With time to think, there would be the possibility that someone else could gain control of the economy, and whoever controlled the economy would be a threat to his power. Hitler would not be willing to make preparations for a world war until forced into them by circumstances.

In the summer of 1936, Hitler inaugurated a short-range four-year economic plan that would lessen German dependency on foreign sources for raw materials and would make the army and the economy ready for his blitzkrieg campaigns. In August 1936, he set forth his goals in a memorandum which he personally drafted.

He wanted Germany to have the finest army in the world within the shortest possible time. The German armed forces and the economy both must be ready for war within four years. But he rejected stockpiling raw materials for a long war. Instead, raw materials should be used immediately for producing munitions and weapons. Germany's economic needs would he satisfied by expanding domestic production and by developing synthetic industries. Costs were irrelevant. Wherever possible, Germany must become 100 percent economically self-sufficient. Foreign exchange would be used only for those materials that could not be produced in Germany.

The aim of this policy was to prepare the German economy for a series of short, hard wars in which Germany's military forces with limited reserves would possess the strength to defeat all enemies. Although the production goals indicated his intention to unleash a series of short wars within a few years, he had not tied himself down to any timetable. Consequently, by 1939, he would have adequate forces for a short war against a smaller nation, but these forces would be inadequate for the major war involving the United States and the Soviet Union that he would be confronted with two years later.

THE FRANCO-SOVIET PACT

One of the peculiarities of the period was the French dependence on treaties, alliances, and pacts. Just as it was characteristic of the Germans to turn to the military, it was characteristic of the French that they sought solutions to their security problems—and perhaps created a few, as well—through alliances. Hitler's renunciation of the disarmament clauses of the Treaty of Versailles brought on talks between France and the Soviet Union that eventually led to the Franco-Soviet alliance. From October 1933, when Joseph Paul-Boncour as French Foreign Minister first proposed a mutual assistance pact to Maxim Litvinov, the Soviet Commissar for Foreign Affairs, until May 1935, when the pact was finally signed, the negotiations took a strange and circuitous path.

After Hitler ordered his delegates to leave the Geneva Disarmament Conference, Paul-Boncour approached Litvinov with the suggestion that, since the Soviet Union had just joined the League of Nations and France had developed an intricate alliance system in Europe, it would be to the advantage of both nations to come to some sort of agreement. Before serious negotiations began, however, Paul-Boncour was turned out of office, along with the rest of the government, because of a political scandal.

The Foreign Minister who took office in February 1934 was a conservative lawyer named Louis Barthou. In continuing the negotiations with Russia, Barthou chose to tie the Franco-Russian alliance to an eastern Locarno Pact—that is, a treaty of regional assistance that would involve the Soviet Union, Germany, Poland, Czechoslovakia, Finland, Estonia, Latvia, and Lithuania. It was shortly before this that Poland and Germany had signed their nonaggression pact, taking both France and Russia by surprise. But it was the Soviet Union that was most alarmed at the event; for Russia had been imagining that it and Germany shared a hostility for the Treaty of Versailles as well as a similar hatred for the Poles. All efforts at international agreement suddenly appeared to be in upheaval. Stalin's attempts to foster better relations with Germany had been rebuffed by Hitler; Germany rejected an eastern European alliance; Poland considered it a blow to its imagined big-power status; France gave up trying to get Germany to disarmament talks; and Italy and Britain were critical of the proposed alliance system. Finally, in September 1934, efforts at achieving an eastern Locarno Pact petered out, leaving Barthou and Litvinov with only the proposed Franco-Soviet alliance.

But, before Barthou could conclude the pact, he was killed in Marseilles when Croatian terrorists assassinated King Alexander of Yugoslavia. Later, a great deal of reverence was paid to Barthou as the only individual who might have been able to stiffen French resistance to Hitler, but such reverence is exaggerated: the revolving cabinet system soon would have pushed him out of office, replacing him with someone less resolute. Actually, Barthou's projects in Europe were insufficient for the needs of France; whatever strengths they possessed would have been dissipated by problems of geography and mutual suspicion among nations.

Finally, it was left to the most unlikely prospect, Pierre Laval, to bring the Franco-Soviet alliance into existence. Laval, a wealthy lawyer who had been a defeatist in World War I, had slight interest in either the eastern alliance system or in any agreement with the Soviet Union. Rather, he dreamed of preserving peace by uniting Britain, Italy, and France in an effort to entice Hitler into a four-power directorate of Europe. When, on March 16, 1935, Hitler wrecked Laval's plans by announcing conscription for building the German army, the French cabinet panicked and forced Laval into concluding the Pact of Mutual Assistance with Russia.

The pact, signed on May 2, 1935, appeared to face Germany with a war on two fronts if either France or the Soviet Union were attacked, but the Franco-Russian security was only on paper. Certainly, each promised the other mutual aid in case of unprovoked attack, but not until both nations had taken the matter to the Council of the League of Nations. Any military action had to wait until they were faced with failure by the Council to reach a unaninious decision. To further complicate matters, action under the terms of the pact could not violate other treaty obligations, such as the Locarno Pact. This meant that, whatever action it was to undertake, France first must have obtained the approval of the Locarno powers—most important, Great Britain. The final fault of the pact was one that Russia hoped to exploit: the band of states that separated Germany from Russia was a barrier to any Russian attack on Germany. The troops of the Soviet Union would have to pass through lands that the czars had once governed. The pact did not indicate how such passage was to be accomplished. France could not be bothered with such a minor problem.

Neither could it be bothered with working out the military details of the pact. Both countries had agreed to a military convention that would determine the tasks of each army, but France seemed to feel that the alliance alone would suffice to divide the German army between east and west, thereby permitting the French troops in the Maginot Line to fend off attacks from a weakened invader. The military details, it felt, were minor matters. But the French reluctance to cooperate with the Russians was not entirely negligence. They had also been put off by Stalin's military purges of 1937 and by the rumors—later proved to have been fabricated by the Gestapo—of Russian intrigues with Nazi generals.

But, if France was unwilling to complete the alliance, it was to the detriment of France. Russia was achieving what it wanted from the pact. In 1935, Stalin had begun to wipe out all opposition to his rule. He accepted the pact because it might give the country limited protection while the internal power struggle raged. His ultimate aim in concluding the pact was to make Hitler more amenable toward making a deal. But, within a year, it became evident that Stalin needed nothing at all from the French alliance. Having tightened his hold on the government of the Soviet Union, Stalin had his emissaries seek to allay German fears that the pact was aimed at encircling Germany.

Actually, the pact proved to be of more use to Hitler than it was to the signatories. Not only did it provide him with the ammunition he needed for his speeches denouncing Russia and communism, but it also aided him in remilitarizing the Rhineland.

THE ANGLO-GERMAN NAVAL AGREEMENT

Britain pursued a different strategy: negotiate a deal with Germany in the belief that intelligent people could always be counted on to come to reasonable agreements. The MacDonald government still sought some form of an arms limitation agreement with Germany, but the best that could be achieved was a naval agreement. Hitler intended to build up the German navy, and in the early stages of this program he wanted British friendship. The negotiation of a naval agreement would reassure Britain that the German fleet would not be a threat. However, the German naval program had begun in 1934, and British naval intelligence lacked hard information about the program. After all, it was easy to keep British naval attachés out of shipyards.

Because an international naval conference was scheduled to meet late in 1935, the British Admiralty wanted exploratory talks with Germany before the conference convened. But Hitler refused to participate in an international naval conference. However, Admiral Erich Raeder, commander in chief of the navy, had hinted to the British naval attaché that Germany would welcome direct negotiations over the strength of Germany's fleet on the basis of an agreed percentage of Britain's fleet. Then, in November 1934, Hitler informed the British ambassador of his interest in a naval agreement with Britain on the basis of about 35 percent of the British fleet When he talked with Simon and Eden in March 1935 he raised the issue of a naval agreement again, stressing that he would stick to the demand for a fleet 35 percent of the tonnage of British fleet. Sir John left Berlin believing that this was Hitler's maximum demand which could be scaled down during negotiations.

The British Admiralty welcomed an agreement, hoping to avoid a naval race similar to that prior to World War I. Moreover, if Hitler's offer were to be rejected, the German fleet might exceed 35 percent of the British fleet. Consequently, such an agreement would help to keep the German navy at a fixed strength in relation to the Royal Navy. With such an agreement it would be easier to distribute the British fleet in the Atlantic and particularly in the Pacific, where the Japanese naval threat was growing. Any reluctance about seeking a naval agreement ended when London learned in April 1935 that Germany was building twelve destroyers, two cruisers, and twelve submarines.

Finally, on June 4, when the representatives of the two governments met in London to negotiate an agreement, Joachim von Ribbentrop, under strict orders from Hitler, refused to make any concessions. The British were either to accept the 35 percent limit or the negotiations would end. After the British gave way on the main point at issue, agreement on the other points was reached quickly.

On June 18, the 120th anniversary of the battle of Waterloo, the AngloGerman Naval Agreement was signed. Germany promised that the total tonnage of the German fleet would never exceed 35 percent of the aggregate tonnage of the combined fleets of the British Commonwealth, and was given the right to build up to 100 percent of the submarine strength of the British Commonwealth. The British had forsaken their insistence on limitation according to category of warship: Germany would not be hampered by restrictions on displacement and gun caliber, insisting on a straight limitation by ratio. Defenders of the agreement rationalized that, since Germany would rearm anyway, the British had to be more accommodating unless they were willing to halt rearmament by force. Any limitation that could be obtained on the German navy would relieve some of the strain on the British fleet spread thin around the world. If Hitler willingly signed an agreement, Britain had little choice but to depend on him to observe it.

They did not realize fully how Hitler had won a brilliant victory. He had managed, by diplomacy, to shatter the Stresa Front and create distrust of Britain among its neighbors. He had succeeded in ending the naval provisions of the Versailles treaty through negotiations and a signed agreement, thereby proving that he could be reasonable. He had succeeded, where the government of Kaiser Whilhelm II had failed, to negotiate a major naval agreement with Germany's major naval opponent. But even further, to Hitler, the agreement revealed British willingness to protect its national interests at the expense of international causes. Most important, the action had created French distrust of Britain, making cooperation between the two countries difficult for some time.

The German victory did not go entirely unnoticed in Britain; but the government was excused from the criticism because the cabinet of Stanley Baldwin was in the process of replacing that of the aged MacDonald and thus could not have had the experience of dealing with such matters. It was the confusion of this transition, some argued, that had allowed them to approve the agreement. But the basis of the arrangement with Germany had been discussed by the two governments before the change. The new cabinet was quite positive in hoping to avoid a repetition of the naval race that had preceded World War I. The agreement would appeal to all who condemned the Treaty of Versailles and longed for armaments limitations. And, since the opposition was much concerned over this subject, an agreement with Germany would aid the government in the coming general election. As for the British Admiralty, it was eager to conclude the agreement in the belief that Germany was voluntarily accepting naval inferiority.

Actually, the agreement did not limit German naval construction as its defenders contended, but then, little would have prevented it were Hitler so inclined. What didn't limit the German navy were inadequacies in the industrial system, the lack of raw materials, and the demands of the German army and air force. The greater naval menace really lay in the Pacific with the Japanese fleet, whose building program Britain could not halt.

With the Anglo-German Naval Agreement, Hitler had finally succeeded in destroying all of the disarmament provisions of the Treaty of Versailles. And he had won his victories without firing a shot. But the succeeding years would prove that Hitler would use his easily gained "military equality" to gain further victories. Europe's years of peace were soon to end.

NOTES
1 Cf. A. J. P. Taylor, *The Origins of the Second World War* (London, 1961), p. 167.
2 Minutes of the Conference of Ministers, February 8, 1933. *Documants on German Foreign Policy,* Series C, I, P. 36.
3 From the word *Sturmabteilung,* the storm troopers.

3 / YEARS OF CRISIS,
1935-1938

MUSSOLINI AND ETHIOPIA

Since 1921, when Poland and Russia made peace, there had been no war involving major European powers. But the peace came to an end in October 1935, when Italian armies sent by Benito Mussolini invaded Ethiopia. Mussolini originally had been an elementary schoolteacher, but his early career also included lecturing on atheism, dodging the draft, and often getting himself thrown into jails for advocating class warfare. His career advanced in 1912 when he became editor of *Avanti*, the official Socialist newspaper, but after he advocated Italian intervention in World War I, he was forced to resign the editorship. He started a new paper, *Il Popolo d'Italia*, and accepted subsidies from the Allied governments, industrialists, and agrarian interests. When Italy went to war, Mussolini was no longer able to avoid the draft. His army record lacked distinction, and he was finally invalided out of the army because of a slight wound from a mortar.

Forsaking socialism in 1919, he founded the *Fasci di Combattimento* (Fighting Group), the Fascist party, which would later terrorize northern Italy. In the fall of 1922, Mussolini, with the help of his party, threatened to overthrow the government. To avoid a civil war, King Victor Emmanuel III surrendered the country to Mussolini. The new dictator was a figure who appealed to businessmen fearful of communism, to frustrated veterans, and to angry nationalists. However, he had no program for government, finding it advantageous to choose his ideology as needs arose.

Mussolini actually lacked physical courage, though he tried to appear to be a superman. He was a notorious lecher and he was also vindictive and cruel, driven by selfish ambition. Musso-

lini was a vain and arrogant man, but often when he met foreigners, he would turn on the charm and they would come away
believing that he was a dynamic leader, resolute in action and
firm in making decisions. Actually he was a fraud, nothing more
than a superstitious peasant fearful of the evil eye, indecisive,
and shaken by fears and prejudices. No one spoke more non-
sense about politics or made more false predictions about foreign
affairs.

He was also naive in his appraisal of Hitler, whom he disliked
as a person but admired as a dictator. Hitler's strength of purpose
and willpower so fascinated Mussolini that he could not bring
himself to question Hitler or to bargain with him. To the bit-
ter end, he believed in Hitler's word. But he was also jealous of
Hitler, and it was his jealousy that drove him into foreign ad-
ventures that Italy could not afford.

Mussolini's foreign policy had no logic, only drift and vac-
illation. He despised Britain and France because their pacifism
seemed weak to him, but he was jealous of their wealth and status.
Childishly, Mussolini dreamed of reestablishing a Roman Empire
around the Mediterranean—a status symbol his dreams told him
he could acquire cheaply and quickly. Ethiopia would be the
first addition. By taking the small African country, he would also
be avenging the disgrace of Adowa, where in 1896, Ethiopian
troops had defeated the Italian army. By succeeding in a short
war with an abundance of military glory, he would be able to
divert the attention of the Italian public from their economic
miseries and impress both Hitler and Europe. He had no qualms
about attacking another member of the League of Nations—
and, at that, a country he had originally sponsored for membership.

He began his preparations for war in 1932, but he had no
excuse to start it until November 1934, when a British commission delimiting the Ethiopian border along the frontiers of
British and Italian Somaliland reached the outpost at Walwal,
inside Ethiopian borders. Since 1930, it had been garrisoned
by Italian forces because of the importance of the nearby wells—
the sources of life in the region. An Ethiopian military force,
which had joined the commission earlier, now set up camp near
the Italian outpost. Because of the tense situation, the commis-

sion withdrew on November 25, leaving the two military forces separated by a line of brushwood about six feet wide. On the afternoon of December 5, shots were fired and a short battle took place. Although the Ethiopians suffered the heavier casualties and fled from Walwal, Mussolini demanded an apology, a heavy indemnity, and the recognition of Italian control of the disputed region. Emperor Haile Selassie was pressured by Britain and France to accede to Mussolini's demands, but he refused, realizing that accession would only encourage Mussolini to make further demands. Instead, the Emperor requested arbitration of the affair, and when Mussolini refused the request, he brought his case before the League of Nations.

The Emperor's action embarrassed the British and French, but more important, it infuriated the Italians, who did not want the League interfering with their bullying. Although the incident was a little ahead of his schedule, it spurred Mussolini to speed up his preparations for war. On December 20, he ordered his generals to prepare Italy for a war of conquest that would commence no later than October 1935.

If there was to be any effective opposition to Mussolini's aggression, it would have to come from Britain or France, which were the only countries with bases in Africa that could be used to mount a campaign against Italy. But the three nations had signed an agreement in 1906 that committed them all to maintain the status quo in Ethiopia and to avoid unilateral action.

Mussolini settled the Ethiopian question with France on January 7, 1935, when he and Pierre Laval signed a formal agreement in an attempt to contain Germany. Mussolini promised to join France in preventing further German rearmament and to maintain Austrian independence, while Laval conceded Italian predominance in Austria. Mussolini surrendered all Italian claims to Tunisia, which France had acquired in 1881, and accepted from France some unimportant portions of North Africa. Then, in an exchange of letters, Laval renounced French economic interests in Ethiopia. More important, in private conversations Laval used the phrase "a free hand," referring, so he later alleged, only to matters economic. Mussolini assumed correctly that this phrase gave him freedom of action in Ethiopia, including the use of force.

On January 29, when he informed Britain of his economic arrangement with France, Mussolini hinted that he had more than a passing interest in Ethiopia. His purpose was to invite the British to discuss the Ethiopian question and to prepare them for the coming war. These overtures were made to Foreign Secretary Sir John Simon, who soon realized that Mussolini was bent on war. Simon had no special liking for Ethiopia. Because of British strategic needs in the Mediterranean, he preferred Italy as a friend rather than an enemy. Simon did not believe that protection of Ethiopia was worth endangering Anglo-Italian relations, and he was certainly not going to risk them by supporting the League of Nations. He could have brought Mussolini to bargain over Ethiopia if he had acted, but, because Simon did nothing, Mussolini interpreted his silence as approval.

An opportunity to set forth the British position on Ethiopia came when Mussolini met with MacDonald, Laval, and Simon at Stresa in April 1935, for the purpose of creating a common front against Germany. Experts on Ethiopia from both London and Paris were present. As the host, Mussolini drafted the agenda from which he omitted any reference to Ethiopia. To be doubly sure, he asked the British delegates to avoid discussing Ethiopia except informally outside the conference room. MacDonald, senile and sick, together with Simon agreed. Their silence allowed Mussolini to claim later that because no formal protest had been made over his Ethiopian policy at Stresa, the British as well as the French had given him a free hand in Ethiopia. Actually, Simon and MacDonald had no policy for Ethiopia, but they gave Mussolini their silent acquiescence in order to get him to join in the Stresa front against Hitler.

The attitude of Simon and MacDonald was supported in Britain by diehard British imperialists, who sympathized with Mussolini, and by a group—led by Robert Vansittart, Permanent Under Secretary in the Foreign Office—who preferred not to antagonize the Italian dictator in hopes of luring him away from Hitler. However, the latter group had exaggerated Mussolini's proprietary concern for Austria. They believed that a Nazi threat to Austria would be resisted by Mussolini, but that proved to be an inaccurate appraisal. Although Mussolini coveted Austria as an Italian satellite, Ethiopia was now more important to him.

He was willing to surrender Austria to Hitler in return for German neutrality in the Ethiopian affair. It is a testament to the Duce's diplomatic ability that he succeeded in fooling the political "realists" into thinking that he might possibly have chosen to ally himself with Britain and France rather than with Nazi Germany.

In June 1935, in Britain, a pioneer effort in sampling public opinion called the "Peace Ballot" was published. Its results were surprising to the "realists" as well as to the other politicians. While it had originated as a means of making Britain more conscious of the League of Nations, its effect was to imply widespread support for the concept of collective security as well as for the League of Nations. Over $11^1/_2$ million people participated in the poll—almost as many as had voted in the general election of 1931. Almost all of those polled were in favor of Britain remaining within the League of Nations and of using economic, nonmilitary sanctions against aggressors. Over $6^1/_2$ million of those polled favored military sanctions (the use of force) if necessary, and only $2^1/_2$ million of them were opposed to military sanctions. Another $2^1/_2$ million abstained from expressing any opinion on the question. The Peace Ballot had the effect of persuading the Baldwin government, which was then facing a general election, to display more enthusiasm for the League of Nations than it had before.

Anthony Eden, minister without portfolio for the League of Nations, traveled to Rome in June 1935 to offer Mussolini a deal—if the dictator would accept only a certain area of Ethiopian territory, Britain would give British territory in Africa to Haile Selassie as compensation. But Eden had come too late with too little. Mussolini scorned the offer, informing Eden that Laval had already given him carte blanche in Ethiopia. Either he would have what he wanted in Ethiopia peacefully or he would take it by force. It is likely that Mussolini had already seen the Maffey report, which had been commissioned in January by the Foreign Office to study British interests in Ethiopia. Although it was not released to the public, Mussolini's agents photographed it in the British embassy in Rome. The report stated: "No vital British interests exist in Ethiopia or adjoining countries sufficient to oblige His Majesty's Government to resist a conquest of Ethiopia by Italy. . . . It is a matter of indifference whether Ethiopia remains independent or is absorbed by Italy."

Having had their bargain rejected, and faced with a general election at home and with Italy preparing for war, the British government decided to take a stand behind the League and in favor of collective security—if all other countries would follow suit. This ingenious solution was the idea of Sir Samuel Hoare, now the Foreign Secretary, who in speaking to the League Assembly on September 11 declared, "The League stands, and my country stands with it, for the collective maintenance of the Covenant, . . . and particularly for steady and collective resistance to all acts of unprovoked aggression. . . . If the burden is to be borne, it must be borne collectively. If risks for peace are to be run, they must be run by all. The security of the many cannot be ensured solely by the efforts of a few, however powerful they may be." This statement made Hoare the hero of all believers in the League's "collective security." His statement, a deception that had the full approval of Baldwin, was aimed at reviving the League sufficiently to intimidate Mussolini into negotiating. Thus, Britain would evade her obligations but still appear to be on the side of the League of Nations.

However, Hoare weakened the effect of his statement by secretly agreeing earlier with Laval that military sanctions—the only action that could deter Mussolini—were too dangerous for Europe. At most, they would be willing to agree to the cautious application of economic sanctions. Hoare went even further in vitiating the impact of his speech by assuring Mussolini, in a personal message on September 23, that Britain had no intention of harming him or interfering with his country's interests and would refrain from applying military sanctions or closing the Suez Canal. Mussolini was now free to begin his war.

On October 3, without a declaration of war, Italy invaded Ethiopia. The League of Nations Assembly met and voted in favor of economic sanctions against Italy, but they left the implementation of the sanctions to the judgment of the League members. Most of the League members did place a ban on all exports to Italy and on most Italian imports but no nation wished to commit itself to more pressure than any other nation. No one dared to suggest blocking the Suez Canal, because the canal fell within British jurisdiction, and Britain did not want to commit itself to such an action. Britain's hesitancy was based on the fear that Mussolini might attempt some foolish act, such as bombing Malta or Alexandria. Since the Chiefs of Staff had advised the cabinet that the fleet in the Mediterranean had insufficient strength to defend itself and that the nation was unprepared for war, Britain would not take provocative action.

Mussolini heightened the fears of the sanctioning nations. He threatened war if Italy were faced with oil sanctions; and his threats were taken very seriously in Paris, where Laval labored on Mussolini's behalf, and in London, where the government realized that no other League member would assist the British navy in enforcing an oil embargo. Mussolini warned the British ambassador that if Italy faced the choice of yielding to sanctions or fighting, it would choose war even if all Europe went up in a blaze. Although on November 14 the Baldwin government did win the general election on a platform of support for the League and for collective security, they had no intention of supporting it to the extent of going to war. Rather, they joined with Laval in seeking a compromise arrangement. British and French diplomats reached a solution early in December. It was with the full approval of the British cabinet that Hoare traveled to Paris to complete the agreement that would leave Haile Selassie with only a fragment of his empire.

Before his departure, Hoare had been repeatedly lectured by Baldwin, "Sam, keep us out of war, we are not ready for it."[1] On December 8, after two days of negotiation, Laval and Hoare initialed the document that is known to history as the Hoare-Laval Pact. It stipulated that Haile Selassie must cede a large portion of Ethiopia to Mussolini; the remainder of the country would become an Italian "sphere of influence." But the provisions of the Hoare-Laval Pact were only proposals which would be worked over in Geneva until all three parties—Italy, Ethiopia, and the League—were satisfied. The negotiators simply wanted to stop the war and let passions cool. But the British cabinet saw the pact as a way to escape a decision on an oil embargo. Consequently the Baldwin cabinet approved the draft and promptly forwarded it to Geneva for League consideration.

When details of the pact leaked from the Quai d'Orsay to the French newspapers, a storm began to gather in the British House of Commons over betrayal of the League of Nations. The uproar so frightened Baldwin that—despite the fact that his government had approved the pact—he forced Hoare to accept full blame for the agreement with Laval and resign from office.

Neither the League nor Haile Selassie would accept the pact, but Laval had achieved his goal—the League's oil sanctions were never enforced. Mussolini's armies completed their conquest of Ethiopia without opposition from any European nation.

Both London and Paris had imagined that the Hoare-Laval Pact could entice Mussolini—by bribing him with Ethiopia— into opposing Hitler. But Mussolini had no inclination to oppose Hitler for Britain and France, whom he loathed. In January 1936, he informed the German ambassador of his appreciation of Germany's benevolent neutrality in connection with the Italo-Ethiopian War; he would have no objection if Austria were to become a German satellite.

Baldwin used the issue of collective security as long as he needed it to win votes; but, once the election was safely past, he demanded peace and appeasement. He feared that sanctions, if truly enforced, would result in war, which neither he nor the nation desired, and he knew he could expect little help from the League of Nations. Also, there was the risk of a quarrel with the United States if British warships stopped American chartered tankers carrying oil to Italy. Although the public voted for collective security, Baldwin knew very well that the public would not support a war over Ethiopia. It was the politicians who had created the uproar over the Hoare-Laval Pact, particularly politicians who had nothing to lose by being indignant over the rejection of Ethiopia and the League. However, these idealists were unwilling to face the truth—that the only alternative to going to war with Mussolini was to make the best possible deal with him.

The movement in Britain in favor of collective security had its greatest support among the liberals, but they were vague about the meaning of "collective security." They never interpreted it to be a military alliance with plans for landing troops in Italy and marching on Rome. Nor did they see it as British soldiers moving into Ethiopia to protect the country from Italian troops.

Instead, they dreamed that it was possible to halt armies by voting resolutions without supporting rearmament.

At the Munich Conference in 1938, Mussolini admitted to Hitler that a strict enforcement of oil sanctions by all the League members would have compelled him to withdraw from Ethiopia within a week. However, if Mussolini really believed his bluff would be met, he was underrating human greed. Despite the oil sanctions, Mussolini would have been able to purchase sufficient oil from the United States and other non-League nations to offset the sanctions. And further, if the British Admiralty attempted to enforce a naval blockade, they would be faced with the possibility of having to sink American tankers carrying oil to Italy.

Mussolini's armies continued the conquest of Ethiopia without interference because none of the members of the League would fight to enforce the Covenant. No nation would go to war over Ethiopia because no nation could feel that its vital national interests were at stake. Therefore, no nation mobilized in behalf of Ethiopia, nor did any nation move troops or ships to aid Emperor Haile Selassie's soldiers—except for the few British ships that were sent to the Mediterranean to watch out for British interests.

The failure of the League members to compel Mussolini to halt his invasion, which was clearly contrary to the Covenant, doomed the League of Nations. Yet the members were not wholly at fault because the challenge presented by the Italo-Ethiopian war had been undreamed of by the authors of the Covenant. They had never expected the League, because of a poorly drawn frontier, to make war in order to defend an African people against a European nation. Of course the League had never been designed as a means of uniting its members in an alliance to halt premeditated aggression.

War in 1935 would not necessarily have prevented the catastrophe that was to come. In fact, it could have precipitated it sooner. For later events were to prove that small preventive wars, instead of halting aggression, only served to bring on more. For example, the German invasion of Poland, by occupying the attention of Britain and France, gave Soviet Russia the opportunity to attack Finland. Had British soldiers battled Italian armies in Africa in 1935, Hitler would have been free to move troops into Central Europe, just as he would do later. As it turned out, the Italo-Ethiopian war, because of the strain on Anglo-French relations, offered Hitler an opportunity to move troops into the demilitarized Rhineland, thereby wrecking the Locarno Pact and ending another restriction in the Treaty of Versailles.

HITLER IN THE RHINELAND

Critics of appeasement have argued that Hitler's aggression should have been halted on March 7, 1936, when he ordered German troops into the demilitarized Rhineland. At that time, they suggest, while Britain and France still had the advantage, he could have been defeated. A display of force, perhaps only a division dispatched into the Rhineland, would have caused Hitler's generals to panic and would have obliged Hitler to recall his troops. Surely a revolution would have followed, he would have been overthrown, and there would never have been a World War II. However, aggression is not halted so easily; and even limited force is subject to escalation.

These critics forget that in 1936, because of guilt over the Versailles treaty and because of the loathing of the war, it would have been an arduous—if not an impossible—task to arouse the British and French peoples to fight a war over German soldiers occupying German territory.

Under the terms of the Versailles treaty, the Rhineland was to be forever demilitarized—no troops and no fortifications. The German government acknowledged this prohibition at Locarno. In his speech of May 21, 1935, Hitler paid his obeisance to the Locarno Pact, implying that he would accept a demilitarized Rhineland. But he was already contemplating occupation, a fact that London and Paris would know in time to plan united action.

After an interview with Hitler on November 21, 1935, André François-Poncet, the French ambassador, advised the Quai d'Orsay that Hitler had condemned the Franco-Soviet Pact and had indicated an intention to retaliate by occupying the Rhineland. On December 13, Hitler went even further by informing the British ambassador that he could easily have occupied the Rhineland in March 1935, but had then been content with maintaining the Locarno Pact. More concrete information on Hitler's intentions followed. Early in January 1936, the Swiss General Staff warned Paris of an impending move by German troops into the demilitarized zone. Two German army corps were also discovered suspiciously close to the demilitarized zone. The information was passed on to the French military attaché in Berlin, who was not surprised: he had suspected that the Germans would occupy the zone; only the date was in doubt.

The signs of military activity along the borders of the demilitarized zone so alarmed the French consul in Cologne that he returned to Paris to report. The rumors were that German troops would be in Cologne within three months, but he also had more concrete information. Military offices, headed by retired officers, were being established in the zone. Housing had been set aside for staff headquarters. In the demilitarized zone, fortifications were being strengthened, gun emplacements erected, barracks prepared for troops, and areas indicated as off limits to civilians. Motorized units of the German army had been moved up to the edge of the demilitarized zone. Every sign pointed to invasion, but no one knew when it might occur. Despite all these threats, the French General Staff did not wish to take any action. Its inertia could be overcome only by strong civilian leadership.

Unfortunately, on January 22, a caretaker government took office until the general election in the spring. It was headed by Albert Sarraut, once Governor-General of Indo-China, a man-about-town and lover of Paris night life, definitely not the person for a critical confrontation with Germany. His Foreign Minister, Pierre Flandin, politely asked for recommendations from the War Ministry in case Germany attempted to alter the status of the demilitarized zone. He hoped that, once acquainted with the military plans, he could talk with London and then send a joint Anglo-French warning to Berlin, thereby forcing negotiation of a solution to the Rhineland question.

But the generals were loath to shoulder the responsibility that ought to have belonged to the civilian ministers. At last, on February 17, Minister of War, General Louis Marin, advised

Flandin and the cabinet that it would be contrary to French interests to occupy the demilitarized zone, because it would make France appear the aggressor, alone and bereft of allies. According to Marin, any French occupation of the Rhineland should be planned only in full agreement with the British. He proposed to alert the troops on the frontiers, to strengthen the fortresses there, and to call up reservists and warn the air force; but he ruled out any French occupation of the demilitarized zone. As an "aggressor," in that case, under the Locarno Pact, France would lose all its allies, including Britain.

On February 19, after the Chiefs of Staff had taken up the matter, General Maurice Gamelin presented their conclusions. If Germany were to occupy the right bank of the Rhine, France must not reoccupy the remainder or even a portion of the area, but must simply take precautionary measures. He advocated keeping the zone demilitarized until France could regain the population it had lost in the years between 1914 and 1918. Although he did not believe that France could prevent Germany forever from doing what it wished with in its frontiers, he believed that they should hold the line until 1940. By February 25, the French War Ministry was sure of what it had been suspecting—that, once the Franco-Soviet Pact had been ratified, Hitler would consider Germany to be free of its obligations under the Locarno Pact; complete occupation of the Rhineland would follow immediately.

Two days later, the Sarraut government came to its decision: French troops would not confront German troops in the Rhineland. French soldiers would not enter the demilitarized zone unless the other Locarno powers dispatched troops. If German forces violated the zone, France would contact the other Locarno powers in order to take concerted action; but, until then, the government could take only precautionary measures. This decision to avoid a confrontation had a practical basis. To bring off an effective confrontation, France required an aggressive, professional military force, ready to sweep into the Rhineland and seize important strongholds while driving out the invaders. But France lacked this kind of army, which could not be trained overnight.

Under the circumstances of 1936, the French General Staff made the only decision possible—to remain on the defensive, man the Maginot Line, and await the German attack that was expected to follow the occupation of the Rhineland. In all truth, the generals had no alternative. Their plans and the training of the troops necessitated such a strategy. The French General Staff, with the approval of the government and the nation, had already written off the Rhineland when they constructed the Maginot Line. This massive defensive complex required that French troops stay within France. Because they had concentrated their efforts on the Maginot Line, the General Staff did not draft plans for an invasion of the Rhineland.

London welcomed French reluctance. The British cabinet, which no longer regarded maintenance of the demilitarized zone as a vital British interest, had been more fearful of the French reaction to a German occupation of the Rhineland than of the occupation itself. The British resented the Franco-Soviet Pact because it gave the Germans an excuse to be unpleasant. They also saw in the pact an indication of a French turn towards Russia and away from Britain. This is not to say that the British wanted an ally, but they wanted the right of veto over French action.

Foreign Secretary Anthony Eden, who had succeeded Hoare, told the French that, because the Rhineland did not endanger British security, the responsibility for the zone lay with the French and Belgians. Rather than fight, Eden preferred to bargain with Hitler over the Rhineland as long as something remained to bargain away. Eden's ideas conformed with those of Prime Minister Stanley Baldwin, who refused any risk, believing that Hitler would not withdraw his troops if they were forced to fight for the Rhineland.

While London and Paris waited, Hitler decided to act. By February 12, he had resolved to occupy the Rhineland. Originally Hitler had set 1937 as the target date for ending the demilitarization of the Rhineland. But because of domestic considerations, he moved the date to 1936. Economic conditions had deteriorated in the Rhineland because German industrialists were reluctant to invest in new plants or to expand and improve older structures. Consequently, the Rhinelanders had not shared in the prosperity connected with German rearmament. Strategically Hitler faced the threat of the Franco-Soviet Pact. Also, the longer Germany delayed entering the zone, the more time its foes would have to increase their military preparations. In addition, for an effective defense against invasion, Germany needed to occupy the Rhineland. For if German forces could not hold the Rhineland, the Ruhr would be endangered— an area vital for the production of German war materials. Reclaiming the Rhineland was a logical step on the path to restoring German power that Hitler promised his generals on February 3, 1933. Moreover, it would vastly improve the operational capability of the German army in any later offensive aimed at the western powers.

If the operation were successful, Hitler's popularity would soar and German security would be strengthened by having German troops on the French frontier. On the basis of military gain alone, the occupation was worth the risk to Germany.

Hitler's decision was also influenced by the attitudes of the Locarno powers. Mussolini promised him that if Germany reacted to the ratification of the Franco-Soviet pact, Italy would not cooperate with Britain and France in any action because of any alleged breach of the Locarno pact by Germany. Furthermore, Britain's military weaknesses were well known in Germany. From London came reports that the Foreign Office was seeking an agreement with Germany despite newspaper stories about the German threat to the Rhineland. France, caught in the depths of economic depression, was facing a general election campaign that would lessen public interest in foreign affairs. For one reason or another, all the major powers who had pledged themselves under the Locarno pact to ensure a demilitarized Rhineland were ready to violate their pledges.

Hitler made it easier for them to violate the treaty by capitalizing on its defects. At the time the treaty was drafted, remilitarization of the Rhineland was considered a prelude to German attack on Belgium and France. Each treaty member was obligated to come to the aid of another if a frontier had been crossed, if hostilities had commenced, or if forces were assembling for an invasion. Hitler, in ordering his troops to occupy the Rhineland, emphasized that they must appear to be peacetime soldiers taking up a permanent garrison in their own country, which indeed they were. To assist the British, Italians, and Belgians in evading their obligations, the appearance of all troop movements must be peaceful with no indication of an impending invasion.

But should this peaceful occupation encounter French forces, what then? The myth still persists, nurtured by the tales told at the Nuremberg trials, that German troops had orders to withdraw if they encountered opposition. It is implied that if French and Belgian forces had merely marched into the demilitarized zone, German soldiers would have immediately retreated without fighting, and Hitler would have been overthrown.

However, this was not the case. The standing orders, in force since Germany left the Disarmament Conference and the League of Nations in 1933, still prevailed: if foreign troops were encountered on German soil, they were to be considered as hostile and were to be repelled. Any withdrawal would be only a strategic retirement to a more defensible line. Hitler had no intention of recalling his troops across the Rhine if French or Belgian troops appeared. Unless he lost his nerve completely, any French resistance could only result in German troops fighting a war to drive out the invaders.

The opportunity Hitler had been waiting for came on February 27, when the French Chamber of Deputies approved the Franco-Soviet Pact. Under orders from Hitler, Marshal Werner von Blomberg, Minister of War, issued the directive for the operation on March 2. Only nineteen infantry battalions and thirteen artillery units, totalling 22,000 regular troops, would enter the demilitarized zone. The national police would be incorporated into the army making a total of 36,500 men. Three infantry battalions, less than 3,000 men, would move further west, one to Aachen, one to Trier, and one to Saarbrücken. At the same time, antiaircraft guns and Luftwaffe fighter squadrons would be moved into the demilitarized zone, but no tanks and no bombers. Marching orders were delayed until the last minute in order to preserve secrecy. Troops within the demilitarized zone were to be positioned so as to protect the Ruhr and to block any French drive eastward to link up with any Czech forces that might cross Germany's eastern border. If France should violate the frontier with any offensive action, the standing orders to defend German soil would take effect. To provide back-up support for the troops within the demilitarized zone, four army corps and thirteen infantry divisions were alerted.

Meanwhile, Hitler's orders to the fleet called for inconspicuous preparations, a submarine reconnaissance, and the equipping of U-boats for action in the English Channel and in the Atlantic. Air defenses were to be strengthened. All of these measures meant that Germany was preparing for war.

Early on the morning of March 7, 1936, advance units of the German army marched into the demilitarized zone. In Berlin at about 10:00 A.M., Foreign Minister Konstantin von Neurath informed the ambassadors from the Locarno powers that Germany was denouncing their pact. In its place, Hitler offered a twenty-five-year nonaggression pact to France and Belgium and an air pact to Britain. He would accept a demilitarized zone only if it were redrawn on both sides of the frontier to give Germany and France equal treatment. For Germany's eastern neighbors, Hitler also had nonaggression pacts. To conclude his offer, Hitler announced his readiness to return to the League of Nations.

By noon, the German national police in the demilitarized zone, having undergone military training for months, were incorporated into the German army. Shortly before 1:00 P.M., the three battalions detailed to the frontier positions crossed the Rhine at Cologne. About the same time in Berlin, Hitler went before the Reichstag to declare Germany no longer bound by the Locarno Pact and to announce that the nation had taken full sovereignty over the Rhineland. At this news, the normally docile members of the Reichstag leaped to their feet, screaming approval and waving their hands in the Nazi salute. When the turmoil subsided, Hitler solemnly vowed not to yield to force and to strive for peace with the western powers. "We have no territorial demands to make in Europe," he declared. "Germany will never break the peace."[2] These were the words that Europe longed to hear.

Since the early in the 1930s, the occupation of the Rhineland had been anticipated by the French government. Precise information had begun to arrive weeks before the coup. French intelligence sources advised the government that France would face a crisis in the demilitarized zone soon after the Chamber of Deputies ratified the Franco-Soviet pact. The French general staff deliberately distorted intelligence to serve its own purposes in order to justify the army's opposition to any offense into western Germany. The French army and air force claimed that they could not move without full mobilization, deliberately exaggerating the German menace. After March 7, 1936, there was no chance that the French armed forces would move. A national election was in the offing, the franc was in trouble, and France was isolated diplomatically. Britain would not help, and neither would the United States nor the Soviet Union.

Faced at last with the crisis that they had been expecting for months, the French politicians and the generals wasted five days in confused debate, and nothing was decided. The politicians refused to accept responsibility for ordering an invasion of the Rhineland. Because the French generals had convinced themselves that Germany had the advantage in numbers (which was not the case) and that any French invasion to end the occupation would mean a general war (which was the case), they reaffirmed their decision not to invade. They dreaded a repetition of the 1914–1918 slaughter of French troops in mass attacks. However, they asked for general mobilization of the army in case a struggle should be forced upon them.

The French generals' request for a general mobilization has been denounced by their critics, but the generals had a legitimate case. For, in peacetime, the standing French army was only a skeleton force that had to be filled out with reservists to make the French army capable of fighting a war. This, too, was the reason that a force could not be hastily assembled from the standing army for an invasion of Germany. No units were ready to go into action intact until after the reservists had been mobilized. France not only had no force capable of immediately occupying the demilitarized zone, it had no unit ready for combat.

France was unprepared for war. Budget cuts in previous years had left the army short of modern equipment. There were critical shortages in modern tanks, anti-tank weapons, artillery, and every type of transport vehicle and communications equipment. The French armaments industry was unable to handle orders for military equipment which had been placed in 1934–35. Because of the lack of material and funds, maneuvers had to be cancelled in 1935. The air force had outdated equipment. The planes that had been ordered would be outdated in a few years. The aircraft industry could not cope with the orders. French military weaknesses only made the German armed forces look all the more terrifying.

Because the French cabinet was marking time until the general election, it did not want to order mobilization. And, too, the cabinet remembered the failure of their unilateral action in 1923, when French troops had occupied the Ruhr to collect reparations. Then, London had disapproved; and, in 1936, London was offering no encouragement for a military action but was calling for negotiations over British and French rights in the Rhineland while they still had negotiating value. Unwilling to run the risk of incurring British censure again, the French cabinet ordered preparations to repel only a German attack on French territory, an attack which would never come.

Had there been an attack, some observers have argued that the French advantage in numbers of trained reserves would have meant Hitler's defeat. But they have exaggerated the possible effectiveness of these troops, forgetting that they were not all immediately available on March 7; and, too, numbers mean little without the will to use them boldly—a quality the French High Command lacked. Furthermore, the French army, untrained for a swift counterattack, would have needed time to mobilize and take up positions; and, while the French were mobilizing, the German forces would have had more time to increase and reinforce their hold on the Rhineland.

War surely would have come if French troops had entered the Rhineland; and the French High Command—which had written off the Rhineland long before March 7, 1936—would have been more defeatist than it was to be in 1940. And, if war had broken out then, French unity would have been severely strained, with voices on the right denouncing the war because it placed France on the side of Russia, and with pacifists on the left condemning a war whose purpose was to drive German troops out of German lands. More important to the French cabinet and generals, France would have been isolated. Only Czechoslovakia promised all-out support while other allies would come to the aid of France only if it were to become a victim of unprovoked aggression.

On learning of the occupation, Eden indicated immediately that Britain would veto any French march into the Rhineland and would devote every effort to mediating between the belligerents. Actually relieved that the long-dreaded crisis had finally occurred, he was determined that it would be met without confrontation between France and Germany. He was following the lead of Baldwin, with whom he agreed, and who rejected every action that risked involving Britain in war. When Flandin personally proposed that Britain should support France in a police action, Baldwin replied: "You may be right, but if there is even one chance in a hundred that war would follow from your police operation, I have not the right to commit England. England is not in a state to go to war."[3] Baldwin's inaction met no protest from the House of Commons. Nor was he troubled by the average British voter, who had no appreciation of the significance of what was happening in the Rhineland. The British "man-on-the-street" could see only that Germany was reclaiming its own territory.

On March 5, 1936, the British cabinet had decided that neither Britain nor France was in a position to take any effective military action against Germany in the event of a violation of the Treaty of Locarno. On March 11, the chiefs of staff had warned the cabinet that most of the British armed forces were concentrated in the Mediterranean watching Italian forces. It would take time to bring them back. The troops that Britain could spare were meager—two infantry divisions who would not be ready until three weeks after hostilities had begun. These two divisions would be dependent upon horses for transportation; they lacked tanks and anti-tank guns as well as infantry mortars. Fearful that the French might act aggressively, the British cabinet on March 11 unanimously rejected any sanctions against Germany, proposed by Pierre Flandin, the French premier, lest it lead to war with Germany, because Britain was unprepared for war. Instead negotiations ought to be initiated with Hitler for a general European settlement.

Because this action was so defensible, Hitler would not have recalled his troops. After committing the armed forces, a retreat would appear to the German people to be a betrayal and an admission of weakness. Had Britain and France fought in 1936, there is no indication that Hitler could have been overthrown by a revolt. The German people—even those Germans who disliked nazism—would have rallied behind Hitler in defense of the Fatherland, for his defense of German soil would have improved Hitler's image as a German patriot.

French Foreign Minister Flandin, confronted with the threat of an aroused Germany, with the handicap of reluctant French generals, and with no allies, decided to ask Hitler to evacuate the Rhineland while negotiations got underway. It would be understood that the result of the negotiations would be full German control of the Rhineland. Such a temperate policy delighted London, but the government in Paris vetoed Flandin's proposal without recommending a reasonable substitute. Finally, on March 19, the League Council assembled in London and condemned Germany's action as a violation of the Treaty of Versailles and the Locarno Pact; and with that action, the Council washed its hands of the matter. On the same day, the Locarno powers officially requested that Hitler stabilize the size of his occupation forces while presenting his case to them. If he would cooperate with them, the Locarno powers—minus Italy—would negotiate his demands, officially revise the status of the Rhineland, and even draft a mutual assistance pact. When Hitler refused to negotiate, he was confronted with no further opposition.

With the remilitarization of the Rhineland, Hitler had demolished the last of the Versailles restrictions on Germany and had struck another blow at the French security system. By permitting German troops to enter the Rhineland unopposed, France had surrendered a vital military advantage. In addition, France had given carte blanche to Hitler to do whatever he wanted with French allies—if France would not fight when its own frontiers were threatened, it was unlikely that French troops would invade Germany when Poland and Czechoslovakia were under attack. Alarmed at French inaction in the face of the sudden growth of German power, the Belgian government chose permanent neutrality, rejecting military cooperation with France, a policy that had been followed since 1920. In April 1937, Belgium was freed of all obligations under the Locarno Pact.

For France, the Rhineland occupation was the inevitable result of the weakness that had plagued the nation since 1919—the lack of an imaginative leadership. But the fault did not all lie with the French, for the British encouraged French inaction. Although postwar critics of Anglo-French policies have alleged that the Rhineland occupation was the last chance to deal with Hitler without bringing on a general war, this was not actually the case. Police action alone would not have succeeded in driving German troops from the Rhineland. Instead, it would certainly have escalated into a general European war; and, in March 1936, neither the governments nor the people of France and Britain considered the Rhineland worth a world war. Not only was the Rhineland German territory, but, in both nations, there were powerful elements sympathetic to Germany, elements that regarded Hitler as a bulwark against communism and that believed Hitler's activities were simply accomplishing the much-needed revision of the Treaty of Versailles. Because German troops had not violated the French and Belgian frontiers, world opinion would have condemned Britain and France for their invasion of Germany in the same way that world opinion would condemn the military intervention of the United States in Vietnam thirty years later.

THE POPULAR FRONT
AND THE SPANISH CIVIL WAR

As Europe adjusted to the new German power, a fresh political coalition formed in opposition to nazism and fascism appeared to offer hope. Shortly after the signing of the Franco-Soviet Pact, Georgi Dimitrov, Secretary-General of the Communist International, issued orders for all Communist parties to combine with bourgeois democratic parties in a broad Popular Front against fascism. Suddenly, Communist parties everywhere discovered their historical ties with bourgeois democracy. In the United States, American Communists aped the Daughters of the American Revolution by proclaiming their patriotism and their love of Lincoln and Washington. French Communists swore their devotion to the Revolution of 1789. Fearful of suffering the fate of their German comrades, the French Communists utilized the idea of the Popular Front in 1934, successfully making overtures to the Socialists and Radical Socialists to unite with them.

The Communist parties, by opposing fascism and allying themselves with non-Fascist parties, achieved a much needed popularity, which helped to attract new members. But the Popular Front failed to halt fascism, chiefly because the Communists never sincerely supported bourgeois democracy. Although they publicly appeared to back the Popular Front, they did not stop their efforts at undermining and destroying the socialist and democratic parties.

Despite the failure of the Popular Front to defeat fascism, it was successful in duping a large number of people into believing that Stalin was eager to protect bourgeois democracy. However, Stalin had sworn to destroy western capitalism, and he would never willingly have defended it unless he needed it for his own ends. At the time the Popular Front developed, Stalin had begun a purge of his opposition. Knowing that this ordeal would weaken Soviet defenses, Stalin needed some kind of temporary protection. The Popular Front seemed to offer that protection by arousing the West against Germany, by keeping alive resistance to nazism, and by distracting Hitler. Furthermore, the Popular Front could prove so annoying to Hitler that he might be willing to resume ties with Soviet Russia—ties that Stalin wanted.

For the purpose of maintaining the illusion of cooperation with the West, Stalin sent Maxim Litvinov to the League of Nations as his spokesman, to preach sermons on the virtues of collective security. If the western democracies, by practicing collective security, could keep Hitler occupied and away from Russia, Stalin could have the opportunity to destroy his critics, many of whom opposed collaboration with Hitler. Stalin would support the idea of collective security and the Popular Front as long as he could profit from the sacrifices of western nations, but he had no intention of allowing Russian soldiers to invade Germany to protect the capitalists.

The most glorious moment for the Popular Front came during the Spanish Civil War. In July 1936, the legally elected Popular Front government was attacked by rebels led by General Francisco Franco. To defeat the Popular Front, Franco called on Hitler and Mussolini for aid. Both men were delighted at being needed and courted. Hitler sent aid to the Spanish rebels, not for the benefit of Spain, but for the profit of Germany. A

Spanish ally could further hinder the French, obliging them to divide their forces between two fronts, and could interfere with British naval communications in the Mediterranean. In addition, a prolonged civil war in Spain would distract foreign attention from Germany and its growing armaments while Hitler pursued his expansionist policies in eastern Europe. A Spanish government sympathetic to Nazi Germany could also be persuaded to provide submarine bases with access to the Mediterranean and Atlantic. However, Hitler did not have a long-range scheme for changing Spain into a Nazi state. He certainly did not plan to commit Germany to full-scale war in Spain. He simply found the situation advantageous for the moment.

In the early weeks of the conflict, Hitler saved the rebel cause by dispatching transport planes to ferry Franco's troops from North Africa. Before the war ended in 1939—with a rebel victory—over 16,000 German soldiers, airmen, and civilians had served in Spain. Not only did their efforts help bring Franco his victory, but they also provided the Luftwaffe with a laboratory to test planes and bombs that would later serve Hitler well against Poland, Britain, and France.

Mussolini also seized the chance offered by Franco, hoping to expand his sphere of influence in the Mediterranean. He lent his assistance with the expectation that Franco's Spain would be a satellite Fascist state. Furthermore, Fascist victory in Spain would compel France to concentrate fewer troops along the Italian frontier. Also, the invitation to display the prowess of his soldiers and airmen was too great an opportunity for Mussolini to pass up. To secure the support of the Roman Catholic Church in his venture, he maintained publicly that Italy was fighting to prevent the establishment of a Communist government in Spain. Finally, the joint intervention of Italy and Germany in the Spanish Civil War helped lay the foundation for a later alliance with Hitler.

Despite the intervention of German and Italian forces in the Spanish Civil War, Stalin hesitated before aiding the hard-pressed Popular Front government. Although he belatedly committed the Soviet Union to the cause of the Republic, he did not relish the expense, and he never dispatched enough aid to bring victory. Like a bourgeois capitalist, Stalin was willing only to sell

Russian aid for Spanish gold and raw materials, and he deliberately limited the use of the aid—there were never more than 2,000 Russian citizens in Spain, and they had orders to remain out of artillery range. Later, all of those Russians who served in Spain were purged because they had been affected so strongly by the liberal idealism of those men and women who battled Franco's legions, and this kind of idealism was too dangerous for Stalin's regime.

By keeping the war going without achieving victory, Stalin hoped that Britain and France would eventually intervene in Spain, thereby occupying Hitler with a western war. Such a conflict—under the terms of the Franco-Soviet pact—would in no way obligate Russia to battle Germany on behalf of France. For Stalin preferred that others support the Loyalist cause and fight the war, so that he could demonstrate his potential worth to Hitler with whom he desired an understanding over Central Europe.

But Britain and France did not see their policy quite as Stalin wanted them to. In Britain, Conservative opinion regarded Franco as the symbol of order and efficiency. British businessmen, with extensive interests in Spain, believed they would fare better with Franco than with the Popular Front. Both Conservative and Labor parties were divided internally over the Spanish Civil War, but all factions were opposed to direct involvement in the war—although some Laborites recommended aid to the Loyalists toward the end of the conflict. From the beginning of the fighting, the British government insisted on localizing the conflict lest it spread beyond Spain, igniting a larger war.

In France, amid a wave of sit-down strikes that paralyzed the economy, a new government had taken office. Because the new government was the French equivalent of the Popular Front—an unstable coalition of Socialists, Radical-Socialists, and Communists—and because of the geographical proximity between Spain and France, it was natural for the Loyalists to ask France for aid. Sympathetic to the Loyalists, Leon Blum, the Socialist intellectual leader of the coalition, at first agreed to the sale of arms. However, the British government pressured him to change his mind. After more deliberations in Paris and London, the Blum cabinet finally stopped the sale of war materials to Spain.

Although London's attitude had influenced this decision to a certain degree, French public opinion had been more powerful. The Radical-Socialists refused to support aid to the Spanish Republican forces; and their departure from the Popular Front would have wrecked the cabinet, thereby ending Blum's hopes for extensive social legislation. Additional opposition came from French Rightists, who viewed the war as a struggle between communism and Christianity and hoped that a Franco victory would regenerate France after bringing down the Popular Front government. It was this intense opposition to the Spanish government that convinced Blum that he would be risking civil war if he sold munitions to the Loyalists.

Reports of the horrors inflicted on the civilian population by the warring factions gave added strength to those who urged appeasement as a means of avoiding a similar struggle throughout Europe. The German and Italian air assaults on poorly defended Spanish cities appeared to be rehearsals for similar attacks on London and Paris. Because the Spanish cities were reduced to rubble in only a few days of bombing, the French and British were able to envision the destruction of their own vulnerable cities filled with hundreds of thousands of casualties. These fears, implanted here, would be harvested during the Munich crisis in 1938.

For all those who believed the right place to fight fascism was on the battlefield, the Spanish Civil War became a crusade. British left-wing intellectuals and workingmen, German and Italian exiles, World War I veterans, unemployed Frenchmen, assorted Communists and Socialists, and American idealists flocked to join the International Brigades, convinced that they were fighting for democracy. They died believing that by defeating Franco, they would strike at Hitler. But even if Franco had been defeated, neither nazism nor Hitler's rule would have disappeared. Actually, a defeat would have had little effect on Hitler, for Spain had never concerned him as anything more than a means of distracting European attention from Germany and perhaps as a way of involving France in a war with Italy. Like Stalin, he had supplied only enough help to keep the war in progress. Finally, in 1939, when he no longer needed the distraction, and when he was certain that France and Britain would not attempt to stop him if he escalated the war, he dispatched enough help to give victory to Franco.

During World War II, however, Franco showed his gratitude for the help given his cause by double-crossing his benefactors, Hitler and Mussolini, when they tried to cash their promissory notes. In 1940, after France had fallen, Franco scorned their pleas to help them against Britain.

Despite the reluctance of the British and French governments to involve their countries in Spain, the Spanish Civil War did influence their policies. The impact of the Spanish Civil War weakened French foreign policy because a Franco victory would mean the threat of encirclement by a new triple alliance—Germany, Italy, and Spain. In addition, the alliance would endanger communications between France and French North Africa where one-third of the French army was stationed. Consequently, the danger of encirclement made France more dependent than ever on Britain and it necessitated the abandonment of any position in Central Europe.

At the same time, because the Spanish Civil War appeared to be a rehearsal for a general European conflict, it frightened London and Paris into a more frantic search for ways to appease the aggressors. It also reinforced the arguments of the appeasers that nothing must be left undone that might prevent another world war.

APPEASEMENT AND APPEASERS

Since 1945, the word "appeasement" has become a derogatory term to be hurled at any political leader willing to negotiate with an opponent. However, at one time, it was a term applied to a policy that was not only publicly approved, but also praised. Originally "appeasement" did not mean surrendering to a bully's demands nor did it mean that nations must surrender their vital national interests in order to avoid war. Instead "appeasement" meant a reduction of international tensions between states through the removal of the causes of friction. It also meant concessions to disgruntled nations in the hope that the concessions would alleviate their grievances and lessen their tendency to take aggressive action. It was hoped that after the aggrieved nations had been pacified through appeasement, an era of confidence, peace, and prosperity would emerge. Moreover, appeasement would permit a reduction in armaments and consequently lower taxes.

While appeasement has most often been associated with Neville Chamberlain, he did not actually originate the policy, but inherited it from his predecessors. It was not a policy created suddenly in the 1930s to buy off Hitler and Mussolini. It had originated in the minds of those who believed that World War I need never have come and that the outbreak of the war was entirely accidental. They thought that both Britain and Germany shared responsibility for the outbreak of the war—an idea nurtured by revisionist historians who argued that the Treaty of Versailles was unjust and should be revised.

But appeasement also stemmed from a lack of faith in the British cause in World War I and from a firm resolve to prevent another European catastrophe. Those English men and women who looked with favor on the German educational system, on German industrial development, and on German social legislation were inclined to back appeasement. There was no one person or group who can be considered responsible for appeasement. Rather, a combination of forces—the horrors of the trenches, the disillusionment over the Treaty of Versailles, and the reluctance to burden Germany with total responsibility for the war—generated and fostered the policy.

Their guilt feelings over the Treaty of Versailles inclined the appeasers to take a soft line whenever Germany complained about the severity of the treaty restrictions. In the early 1920s, French insistence on complete fulfillment of the Versailles treaty alarmed the appeasers, who feared that France would force Germany to take up arms again. Consequently, they argued that war could be prevented only by nonfulfillment of the treaty terms.

British opposition to the French occupation of the Ruhr in 1923–1924 had the effect of preventing the enforcement of the Treaty of Versailles. At the same time, it rescued Germany from being torn apart by the separatist movements that had begun to develop. When French troops withdrew from the Rhineland, the appeasers, as well as the Germans, had won a great victory;

if France could not enforce the treaty, then it would never be enforced, and without enforcement, revision of the treaty—the appeasers' goal—would be easier.

J. Ramsey MacDonald, who became Prime Minister in 1924, helped clear up the difficulty that resulted from the Ruhr occupation by pushing the Dawes Plan through to completion. Under his leadership, a conference in London in the summer of 1924 brought the French and the Germans together to consider the reparations problem. The nations who met at the London Conference agreed to end the Ruhr occupation and to assist German recovery with a loan—but they refused to help France and Belgium, both of whom had suffered heavier damage than had Germany. With these concessions granted, Germany agreed to pay the reparations at a reduced rate. Because Britain and its allies treated the former enemy as an equal, appeasement became more firmly established.

Stanley Baldwin, who later in 1924 succeeded MacDonald as Prime Minister, was well-acquainted with the habits of the British electorate, but he paid as little attention as possible to foreign affairs, preferring to postpone unpopular decisions on the chance that they would solve themselves. Truly ignorant of foreign affairs and socially uneasy with foreigners, he could neither comprehend nor deal with the impending conflict in Europe, and so resolved on peace at any price. He was well aware of the German breaches in the Treaty of Versailles, but he unhesitatingly accepted the Locarno Pact. It did seem at the time that the final solution to Europe's postwar problems had been reached at Locarno. Many of the appeasers envisioned the treaty as creating a new spirit that would bring peace to Europe. Because Germany had freely participated in a conference and had willingly signed an agreement, the appeasers were convinced that they had replaced the ineffective Treaty of Versailles with an agreement that could be maintained.

When Hitler came to power, the arguments in favor of appeasement increased. Whatever faults the new Germany might possess, the appeasers believed that it could not have been as great a threat as the threat of Communist Russia. They believed that German rearmament should be accepted and changes must be made in the Treaty of Versailles.

By 1937, when Neville Chamberlain became Prime Minister, appeasement had become entrenched as British foreign policy. He was not a naive man as many would want to paint him, but actually a seasoned politician. Son of the famous Joseph Chamberlain, Neville had trained for a career in business. He understood contracts, accounts, and production schedules better than the intricacies of European diplomacy. He was conscientious but lacking in imagination; and his brusque and obstinate manner did not gain him popularity. Convinced that the techniques of business would succeed in international diplomacy, Chamberlain approached Hitler and Mussolini as he would a fellow businessman, offering them deals that would be mutually advantageous.

As a young man, Chamberlain failed at growing sisal on the island of Andros where his father had sent him. Returning to Birmingham, he began a successful business career, entered politics, and was elected to the City Council, finally becoming Lord mayor, a post once held by his father. Next he was elected to Parliament and eventually became Postmaster General, Minister for Health, and in 1931, Chancellor of the Exchequer.

Chamberlain had a key role in the national government during the 1930s. He was the dominant figure in the National Government formed under J. Ramsey MacDonald in 1931 and also in Stanley Baldwin's government. Exerting a strong influence in military policy as well as foreign affairs in both governments, Chamberlain became prime minister in 1937. He had attained his preeminence by hard work and determination, but he did not easily tolerate opposition and criticism. However, he could be flattered as Hitler discovered.

Chamberlain believed that the maintenance of economic stability was the essential element in Britain's defensive strength. To him it was the fourth arm of defense. The strain in the rearmament program, plus warnings from strategists, convinced Chamberlain that the global problems must be relieved by approaches to Mussolini and Hitler. Chamberlain wanted to keep defense spending under control and avoid tampering with the industrial system. Chamberlain was also influenced by senior officials in the government. More often than not, he received mediocre advice. He was too ready to accept whatever he wanted to hear. Too often he sidetracked or excluded his critics. Chamberlain needed opposition to offer a dose of self-criticism which he unfortunately resented.

Distrustful of Foreign Office bureaucrats, he relied too much on his narrow background and on those whose grasp of European affairs was minimal. Men such as Hoare, Simon, Halifax, and Wilson were poor choices for advisors. Both Hoare and Simon had been failures at formulating foreign policy, and Halifax's ignorance of European affairs had made him ill-prepared to be Foreign Secretary. The last member of the quartet, Sir Horace Wilson, was a very capable civil servant, an expert in labor disputes with the title of "Chief Industrial Adviser to the Government," but in foreign affairs he was strictly an amateur. Given an office in No. 10 Downing Street, he acted unofficially for Chamberlain, often presenting his views in behind-the-scenes meetings with German officials.

Chamberlain would not listen to Eden, the Foreign Secretary he had inherited from the Baldwin cabinet. The Prime Minister believed that diplomats wasted time in red tape, and that he must handle his own foreign policy in order to avoid this problem. When he took office, he had resolved to end the policy of drift and inaction that had typified the Baldwin administration; and to do this, he believed he had to act quickly and independently on policy matters. It was to be expected that he would clash with Eden, who preferred more traditional ways of dealing with the fascist powers.

The difficulties between Chamberlain and Eden came into the open over a proposal made by Franklin Roosevelt in January 1938, that the diplomatic corps in Washington meet to consider an agreement on the basic principles of international conduct. This agreement would include decisions on the reduction of armaments, methods of promoting economic security, and measures for protecting neutrals in wartime. Chamberlain objected strenuously to this plan; he was certain that it would not only fail but also ruin all his efforts at appeasement. Without informing Eden of his move, Chamberlain requested Roosevelt to postpone putting his plan into effect. Eden, who thought he saw excellent possibilities in the Roosevelt proposal, had no success in convincing Chamberlain to change his mind. Although he has generally been condemned for rejecting the President's impractical scheme, Chamberlain, because of Roosevelt's previous unwillingness to commit the United States to any international responsibility, had some justification in believing the efforts would come to naught. The only important result of Roosevelt's proposal was to strain the relations between Chamberlain and Eden to the breaking point.

The breaking point came almost immediately—on the question of Ethiopia. In hopes of separating Mussolini from Hitler, Chamberlain wanted immediate discussions over recognition of the Italian conquest of Ethiopia. Eden preferred to negotiate on a quid pro quo basis: Mussolini could withdraw his troops from Spain, and then Britain would recognize the conquest of Ethiopia. When Chamberlain rejected Eden's recommendation entirely, the Foreign Secretary resigned on February 20, 1938.

Edward, third Viscount Halifax, who followed Eden as Foreign Secretary, was much more to Chamberlain's liking. A country gentleman, a former Viceroy of India, and a High-Church Anglican with deep spiritual convictions, Halifax was completely unsuspecting when confronted with individuals such as Hitler and Mussolini. He had never bothered to read *Mein Kampf,* and he believed that those who had warned against Hitler were exaggerating. But this was the person whom Chamberlain wanted as Foreign Secretary—a faithful servant of the King who would not object to whatever brand of appeasement Chamberlain wanted to practice.

Before he took office, and despite the protests of Eden, Halifax was sent on his first errand for Chamberlain. In November 1937, Halifax accepted an invitation from Hermann Goering to attend the Sporting Exhibition in Berlin. On November 17, the English country gentleman met with Hitler at Berchtesgaden; but he almost wrecked the meeting at the outset by mistaking Hitler for a footman, stopping short of handing the dictator his hat. Halifax was in agreement with Hitler on the inequity of the Treaty of Versailles, but he wanted the potentially dangerous questions arising from the treaty—Danzig, Austria, Czechoslovakia—handled in a peaceful way. He promised that the British government would not "block reasonable settlements . . . reached with the free assent and goodwill of those primarily concerned."[4] This was just short of an invitation for Hitler to do whatever he wanted in Central Europe. Hitler had already—in the Reichschancellery meeting—announced plans for expansion; but now, thanks to Halifax (and Chamberlain), he had the means for taking the territory he wanted. If he could make his moves appear to be in accordance with the wishes of the people in the territories occupied, he would have British consent.

The policy that resulted in this invitation to Hitler had developed considerably since Versailles. In retrospect, appeasement had so managed to root itself into British foreign policy as to make it extremely difficult—if not impossible—for Chamberlain to have taken any other approach. Under Lloyd George, with his attempts to make Wilson lighten the Treaty of Versailles, appeasement became the keystone of British foreign policy. All of Lloyd George's successors followed his example: Andrew Bonar Law denounced the French occupation of the Ruhr in 1923; MacDonald, in his first administration, got the French out of the Ruhr, and in his second administration, preached disarmament of Britain and its allies as a means of satisfying German complaints about military inequities; and Baldwin aided the growth of appeasement by making the Anglo-German Naval Agreement the crowning diplomatic achievement of his third government.

By the time Chamberlain came to office in 1937, appeasement would no longer satisfy Hitler (whom Chamberlain regarded as a German politician with strong feelings about the Versailles treaty and the suffering German people). Nevertheless, Chamberlain prescribed a more vigorous form of appeasement than had his predecessors, pushing for intensive discussions and, if necessary, face-to-face negotiations between heads of state. Appeasement to Chamberlain did not mean surrendering to Hitler's demands, however, but it meant finding ways of satisfying those demands by wise concessions that would avoid further dangers to peace. Chamberlain honestly believed that world peace could be guaranteed by economic prosperity, by ending existing economic difficulties; and he believed that these troubles could be solved by reducing military expenditures and by balancing national budgets. Germany, he believed, would become more peacefully inclined if southeastern Europe were opened to German economic exploitation, thereby ridding the country of the need for a massive army and providing the German economy with a market. This fact has often been minimized in evaluating the years before the war. For Chamberlain practiced appeasement, not out of cowardice or fear, but out of a positive belief that appeasement would open the way to peace for all.

Chamberlain did not deliberately appease Hitler in order to turn his aggressive activities away from the West and toward the Soviet Union—Chamberlain was not as cunning as that. True, he distrusted the Russians, but he feared that another world war would devastate Europe and leave Communists in control. To Chamberlain as well as the other appeasers, the greatest evil of all—the evil to be avoided at all costs—was war. One world war was sufficient to make the appeasers fearful of what the outcome of such a major conflict might be.

The appeasers did ignore one important fact: a policy of appeasement could end only with Germany restored to its former strength. Given the German population, industry, educational system, and—above all—geographical position, appeasement had to result in German domination of Central Europe and perhaps in an attempt to dominate all of the Continent as well. The appeasers' sins were the sins of all of the post-1919 generation, who read Keynes, regretted the Treaty of Versailles, sorrowed for Germany, and admired Mussolini for running trains on time. They took too optimistic a view of the Germans, always conceding the benefit of the doubt in hopes of bringing peace. Through improved Anglo-German relations, they sought to avoid direct conflict. Although they would later be reviled for their actions, the appeasers did perform a vital task: their efforts for peace proved without a doubt that Hitler could not be trusted and eventually convinced Britain that war was necessary and just.

NOTES
1 Thomas Jones, *A Diary with Letters 1931–1950* (London, 1954), p. 158.
2 William L. Shirer, *Berlin Diary* (New York, 1941), pp. 51–54.
3 Winston Churchill, *The Gathering Storm* (Boston, 1948), p. 197.
4 Lord Birkenhead, *Halifax* (London, 1966), p. 370.

4 / THE ROAD TO WAR, 1938

On November 5, 1937, Hitler summoned a select group of ministers and military leaders to a meeting in the Reichschancellery. In the history of Nazi Germany, this meeting has come to have a great deal of significance because it seems to have indicated deliberate planning for another world war. If Hitler had plans for European conquest, his staff needed to be informed, for they were not simply party hacks but included Hermann Goering, Commander-in-Chief of the Luftwaffe; General Werner von Fritsch, Commander-in-Chief of the army; Konstantin von Neurath, Foreign Minister; Field Marshal Werner von Blomberg, Minister of War; Admiral Erich Raeder, Commander-in-Chief of the navy; and Colonel Friedrich Hossbach, Hitler's military adjutant. Hossbach has contributed to our knowledge of this meeting by making an unofficial record reconstructed from notes made during the meeting. Hitler called the conference because of a quarrel among his staff: Blomberg had complained about Goering's rapacity in acquiring raw materials for the Luftwaffe. The conference gave Hitler the opportunity to push his personal plans by discussing the expansion of the armed forces and rearmament within the context of foreign policy. In addition, he resolved to use the conference to prod Fritsch into accelerating the expansion of the army. Hitler also sought to impress on his audience, particularly Fritsch and Blomberg, that Germany's future in Europe demanded an increased speed-up in rearmament.

To impress his audience, Hitler announced that his words were to be considered his last will and testament. He asserted that the problem of German living space had become a crisis; complete self-sufficiency would not supply all Germany's needs for raw materials and food. He insisted that the solution to this problem lay in acquiring living space in the countries surrounding Germany. Because rearmament was nearly complete and any delay in solving the problem of living space would mean greater obsolescence in equipment, Germany must take the offensive before other nations finished rearming. Each year the nation's leaders would grow older, and the Nazi party would lose its momentum, while the threat of a lower standard of living would increase as the population continued to grow. Asserting that he had no choice but to act, Hitler vowed to solve Germany's problem of living space no later than 1943–1945.

In the short term, he looked to the south and the east. The incorporation of Czechoslovakia and Austria into Germany, Hitler argued, would provide the Fatherland with a more defensible frontier and with new sources of manpower, raw materials, and food. Further, if France should continue to be embroiled in internal problems, Germany could move against Czechoslovakia, and it seemed likely that Britain would not permit France to attack Germany. But if Germany should become involved in a war with Britain and France, Czechoslovakia and Austria would have to be overthrown simultaneously to protect the eastern flank. Once Czechoslovakia had been defeated, Hitler expected, Poland would be passive.

However, Hitler firmly believed that Britain and France had already written off Czechoslovakia and that neither Italy nor Russia would be sufficiently concerned to intervene. He brazenly predicted that, in any case, France would be unable to act against Germany because, by the summer of 1938, both France and England would be too busy fighting with Italy in Spain. Consequently it would be in Germany's interest for the Spanish Civil War to continue.

Hitler's pronouncements provoked sharp questioning from Fritsch and Blomberg, who opposed taking any action that might place Britain and France in the position of becoming Germany's enemies. Hitler retorted that under no circumstances would Britain be likely to join in a war against Germany; and, without British backing, they could be assured that France would be afraid to take any action. But the generals warned that, should there be such a conflict, Germany would not be entirely in the clear, because France would still possess sufficient troops to have superiority on the western front. Blomberg argued that mobilization in France had proceeded further than it had in Germany, that the western German defenses were inadequate, and that the motorized divisions of the German army would not be able to fulfill the tasks they would be given. Blomberg also worried over the strength of the Czechoslovak fortifications, which had been modeled on the Maginot Line. This problem was so important, Fritsch contended, that he had already ordered a special study of methods to breach these fortifications. He proposed to cancel his leave, which he had planned to spend abroad, but Hitler assured him that war was not imminent. Neurath expressed doubt that an Anglo-French-Italian conflict, predicted by Hitler, would be likely to break out so soon. Hitler stood by his assertion that war seemed possible in the summer of 1938. When these hostilities commenced, he wanted German forces to attack Czechoslovakia. According to Hossbach's memorandum, the argument subsided with the remainder of the conference devoted to a discussion of the armaments and raw materials problems, which had been the original excuse for the conference.

In assessing the significance of this conference, Hitler's remarks must not be dismissed simply because his predictions about the Spanish Civil War proved inaccurate. Hitler was neither daydreaming nor attempting to fool his audience. He knew he could accomplish little without their cooperation. He was neither prophesying not planning, but was describing opportunities that Germany should be ready to exploit. He had confessed to his audience that he no longer would limit his actions to ending restrictions remaining in the Versailles treaty, but instead would seize lands never ruled by the Hohenzollerns. His goal now was conquest, not treaty revision.

However, the conference also proved to have served another purpose, for three of the audience—Fritsch, Blomberg, and Neurath—were soon relieved of their positions. These three officials did not question Hitler's goals but only the risks. They disputed Hitler's assessment that the conflict would be limited to Germany and Czechoslovakia and would not escalate into a more general war, with Britain and France fighting in support of Czechoslovakia.

Blomberg, evidently more disposed towards obeying his Fuehrer than were the others, obediently took steps to implement the new goals, but this did little to ward off his dismissal. He approved a new directive, dated December 21, 1937, to alter an earlier strategic plan known as *Operation Green,* which had been intended for a war on two fronts with the emphasis on the southeast. Although new plans had to be worked out for Hitler's offensive war, *Operation Green* would be used in case a favorable situation should develop in the meantime. It called for German armed forces to occupy Bohemia and Moravia speedily, leaving only a minimum force for security in the west. A surprise attack would be launched before the Czechoslovak forces mobilized, and the bulk of the Luftwaffe would be committed against Czechoslovakia.

Those who drafted the directive had grasped the meaning of the Reichschancellery conference: Czechoslovakia would be the first target because potentially it was stronger than Austria. Yet when Hitler was presented with the opportunity, he would take Austria first.

In the aftermath of the Reichschancellery Conference, Hitler found an opportunity to purge the High Command. Blomberg, the first to go, made Hitler's task easy. On January 12, 1938, with Hitler and Goering as witnesses, Blomberg married Eva Gruhn, a stenographer with a police record involving posing for pornographic pictures. After Goering made Hitler aware of Frau Blomberg's police record, the Fuehrer seized the opportunity to force the retirement of her husband from the Army. At the same time, he used a trumped-up charge of homosexuality, which he knew to be false, to rid himself of Fritsch, who as senior general would be in line to succeed Blomberg as War Minister. Through these actions Hitler strengthened his position and, at the same time, weakened the independence of the military leadership.

Goering, who had helped bring down Blomberg and Fritsch, coveted the post of Minister of War. Hitler, who feared giving any one person too much power, rejected him because Goering already commanded the Luftwaffe and headed the Four-Year Plan. Instead, Hitler abolished the office of Minister of War, creating in its place the *Oberkommando der Wehrmacht* (OKW—High Command of the Armed Forces) headed by a chief of staff, General Wilhelm Keitel, a submissive character, completely under Hitler's spell. At the same time, Hitler would become the Supreme Commander of the Armed Forces with the OKW as his military secretariat.

To succeed Fritsch as Commander-in-Chief of the Army, Hitler chose General Walter von Brauchitsch, who was about to retire from the Army because of his marital troubles. Hitler bribed him with a financial settlement which enabled him to extricate himself from his first marriage and then marry the woman with whom he had been living, who was an ardent admirer of the Fuehrer. As part of the deal, Brauchitsch had to promise to move the Wehrmacht closer to the state and to the Nazi ideology. He also had to accept the retirement of a number of generals and the reassignment of others to new commands. To soften Goering's disappointment, Hitler promoted him to the rank of Field Marshal. These changes were all announced on February 4, including the appointment of Joachim von Ribbentrop as Foreign Minister, replacing Neurath, another Hindenburg choice. Three ambassadors were replaced: Ulrich von Hassell from Rome, Herbert von Dirksen from Tokyo, and from Vienna, Franz von Papen. Altogether, these changes gave Hitler greater control over those areas vital to securing the objectives he had discussed in the Reichschancellery meeting. He had succeeded in ridding himself of those in high office from whom opposition could be anticipated, and he had replaced them with individuals who were both acquainted with and prepared for the route Hitler was traveling. At the same time, his actions undermined the independence of German military leadership and strengthened his control over the armed forces.

THE ANSCHLUSS

Although Czechoslovakia was supposed to be the main target according to Hitler's Reichschancellery pronouncement and the Wehrmacht directive of December 21, the opportunity to take Austria occurred first. A desire for *Anschluss* (union of Germany and Austria) had created controversy in the years since 1918. As early as the closing months of World War I, when the Imperial German armies were retreating before the advancing Allied forces, General Erich Ludendorff pressed the Foreign Ministry to seek *Anschluss* to soften the sting of defeat, but the more

Top: The Council of Four which dominated the Paris Peace Conference in 1919.
(Left to Right) British Prime Minister David Lloyd George, Italian premier
Vittorio Orlando, French Premier Georges Clemenceau and American President
Woodrow Wilson. *U.S. Army Signal Corps photograph reproduced courtesy of the
George C. Marshall Research Library*

Bottom: Benito Mussolini and Adolf Hitler in automobile, Munich, 1940.
Courtesy National Archives

Top: The Reichstag cheering Hitler on March 13, 1938, at the announcement of the union of Germany and Austria. *AP/Wide World*

Bottom: Edouard Daladier, French premier, 1938–1940, nicknamed "the Bull of the Vaucluse." Someone commented that "this young bull smells of the stable." *Courtesy National Archives*

Top: Edward, third Viscount Halifax, the country gentleman whom Neville Chamberlain chose to be foreign secretary. *Courtesy U.S. Department of State*

Bottom: The Munich Conference, September 29–30, 1938. From left to right, Neville Chamberlain, Edouard Daladier, Adolf Hitler, and Benito Mussolini. *AP/Wide World*

We, the German Führer and Chancellor and the British Prime Minister, have had a further meeting today and are agreed in recognising that the question of Anglo-German relations is of the first importance for the two countries and for Europe.

We regard the agreement signed last night and the Anglo-German Naval Agreement as symbolic of the desire of our two peoples never to go to war with one another again.

We are resolved that the method of consultation shall be the method adopted to deal with any other questions that may concern our two countries, and we are determined to continue our efforts to remove possible sources of difference and thus to contribute to assure the peace of Europe.

A. Hitler

Neville Chamberlain

September 30. 1938

Top: Neville Chamberlain at Heston Airfield, September 30, 1938, waving the statement that he and Adolf Hitler had signed in Munich. *AP/ Wide World*

Bottom: The statement signed in Munich by Chamberlain and Hitler, September 30, 1938. *Courtesy National Archives*

Left: Vyacheslav Molotov, Soviet Commissar for Foreign Affairs, signing the Nazi-Soviet Non-Aggression Pact in Moscow, August 23, 1939. Standing immediately behind him are Joachim von Ribbentropp, German Foreign Minister and to the right Joseph Stalin, General Secretary of the Communist Party. *AP/Wide World*

Below: The Nazi Hierarchy: Hitler with Goering, Goebbels, and Hess. *Franklin D. Roosevelt Library, Courtesy National Archives*

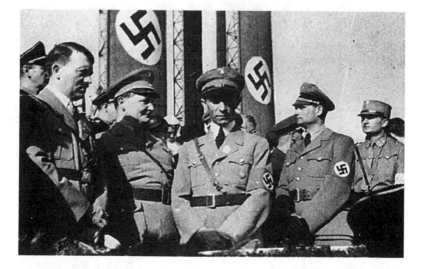

Above: German soldiers try to dislodge snipers in Warsaw during the Nazi invasion of Poland in September 1939. *AP/ Wide World*

Right: A somber Neville Chamberlain leaves No. 10 Downing Street to attend a special meeting of parliament on September 1, 1939 after German troops had invaded Poland. *AP/Wide World*

responsible ministers refused to endanger the delicate peace
negotiations with such a provocative act. Envisioning such a
threat, Clemenceau insisted on inclusion of Article 80 in the
Versailles treaty, prohibiting *Anschluss* unless approved by the
Council of the League of Nations.

During the 1920s, the feeling for union between the two
countries was stronger in Austria than in Germany. Agitation
in certain Austrian areas led to unofficial plebiscites, which carried overwhelmingly in favor of *Anschluss.* Although the Versailles
powers eventually found it necessary to order the cessation of
these movements, by 1930 the depression had stirred up Austrian sentiment for *Anschluss* as the way to revive the economy.
At this time, the government in Berlin was desperate for some
foreign policy victory to counter the growing Nazi accusations
that the Weimar Republic had given in too easily at Versailles.

On March 21, 1931, after secret discussions, the Austrian and
German governments suddenly announced that they had agreed
on a projected customs union, which would remove all trade
barriers between Austria and Germany and create an economic
Anschluss. Because they had feared opposition, the two governments had not discussed the plan with other governments before making the public announcement, as was customary in cases
of agreement that might alter the balance of power. Apprehen-
sive that these new economic ties might ultimately lead to complete *Anschluss,* the western powers, under French prodding,
protested vehemently. France forced Austria to withdraw from
the scheme by threatening to block a vitally needed loan. Because of the collapse of the Kreditanstalt, liquid capital was sorely
needed in Vienna; and so, Austria gave in.

The World Court had the final word in the matter in September 1931, when it held that the customs union endangered the
economic independence of Austria. The defeat of the customs
union deprived the Weimar Republic of a sorely needed triumph
over the Versailles powers to offset the growing strength of the
Nazis. But the opponents of *Anschluss* were correct in assuming
that it was not the answer to the economic needs of Germany
and Austria. What was needed in Europe then was a Common
Market, but this was too radical a solution for the time.

The *Anschluss* movement was renewed when Hitler came to
power. The Fuehrer had never concealed his sentiments on the

matter. They were spelled out clearly on the first page of *Mein Kampf,* and he never retracted his statements. He gave the incorporation of Austria into the greater Nazi Germany a prominent place in his program; and within Austria, he was aided by an active Nazi party that lived only for the day when Austria would be able to join the Third Reich.

After the debacle of July 1934, Hitler had to alter his tactics. Instead of depending on a successful coup by the Austrian Nazis, the Fuehrer had to try diplomacy to achieve *Anschluss.* He dispatched Franz von Papen to Vienna as the German minister with orders to patch up relations with Austria and to promote *Anschluss.* After prolonged negotiations, Papen convinced Austrian Chancellor Kurt von Schuschnigg to accept an Austro-German agreement. Because there was no alternative, on July 11, 1936, Schuschnigg signed. Austria had possessed no allies who would come to its aid against an economically and militarily powerful Germany. Hoping that the agreement would ease tension between the two countries and lift part of the burden on the Austrian economy, Schuschnigg accepted the German demands.

The published text of this agreement seemed innocent; but it actually represented capitulation of Austria to Hitler. Germany recognized the full sovereignty of the Austrian government, both countries pledged noninterference in the internal affairs of the other, and Austria acknowledged that it was a German state; but the real agreement, which contained a great many advantages for Germany and few for Austria, was kept secret. According to this document, Austrian Nazis would be free from harm as long as they complied with the laws of Austria. Both Germany and Austria renounced the use of radio, motion pictures, newspapers, and the theater for propaganda purposes. Both countries removed all restrictions on the sale of books from the other country. Five newspapers from each nation would be permitted circulation within the other. Germany promised to lift economic restrictions on trade as well as tourism—a concession important to Austria. Schuschnigg agreed to conduct Austrian foreign policy to conform to the policies of Germany and to grant political amnesty to imprisoned Austrian Nazis. Finally, and most significantly, he promised to invite leaders of the opposition

(Nazis or those sympathetic to nazism) to join his movement. The agreement of July 11, devised to achieve *Anschluss* by evolution, was like a leash tightened by Berlin to strangle slowly Austrian independence. Although hidden from the rest of the world, the agreement was divulged to the Austrian Nazi leaders, who were ordered by Hitler on July 16 "to work for the *Anschluss* through the July 11 Agreement."[1]

In operation, the agreement proved to be quite detrimental to Austria. The newspapers and books from Germany were crammed with Nazi propaganda critical of the Austrian government, and any Austrian censorship of these publications would have violated the July agreement. If the Vienna government dared to enforce the civil laws against Austrian Nazis, Berlin would accuse Schuschnigg of violating the agreement. To comply with the agreement, Schuschnigg had to admit friends of the Nazis into his government, so he appointed Odo Neustaedter-Stuermer and Edmund Glaise-Horstenau. In 1937, Schuschnigg appointed Arthur Seyss-Inquart, whom he thought he could trust to be fairly moderate, but Seyss-Inquart was soon in communication with German officials and became the leader of those Austrian Nazis who sought a peaceful union with Germany.

Despite the agreement, Austro-German relations continued to deteriorate. On May 2, 1937, when the Austrian police raided the headquarters of the Nazi party in Vienna, they found material indicating collaboration between the German and Austrian Nazi parties. There were records of talks between Austrian Nazi leaders and Hitler, propaganda hostile to the Austrian government, evidence that the German government supplied funds to Austrian Nazis, and records of a courier service between the Austrian and German Nazi organizations. When confronted with this subversion, Papen responded by attacking Schuschnigg for exhausting Hitler's patience by his failure to keep the agreement.

When Hitler discussed Austria at the Reichschancellery meeting on November 5, 1937, it is significant that he no longer talked about an evolutionary policy for *Anschluss* but actually spoke of "attacking" Austria. Although Hitler feared Czechoslovakia more than he feared Austria at this date, because of a combination of chance and human error, Austria would prove to be the first nation his forces would occupy. Another raid on the Austrian Nazi party headquarters in Vienna on January 25, 1938, uncovered plans for a Nazi coup, but Schuschnigg refused to publish these documents because he feared that they might antagonize Hitler. According to the plans, Austrian Nazis, by resorting to riots and acts of sabotage, would provoke the Austrian government into deploying troops to restore law and order. Berlin would then send an ultimatum demanding the withdrawal of the troops and the incorporation of the Nazis into the Austrian government; once inside the government, they could then begin the take-over. If the Schuschnigg government rejected the ultimatum, it would be violating the July 11 agreement, and Hitler would have an excuse for an invasion. It is uncertain whether Hitler knew of the existence of these plans; but, had the coup come about and presented him with a chance for *Anschluss*, there is no doubt that he would have seized it.

Despite the discovery of these plans, Schuschnigg continued his struggle to pacify the Nazis while trying to govern Austria, but it became more difficult daily. Hoping that a meeting with Hitler would help to calm the more militant Austrian Nazis, Schuschnigg, in early January 1938, accepted an invitation from Hitler for a meeting on January 26. However, because Hitler had become involved in the crisis over the army High Command, he postponed the meeting to mid-February. To create a favorable atmosphere for the meeting with Hitler, Schuschnigg commenced negotiating Austrian Nazi demands. But in the process of negotiating, he granted concessions he could ill afford. These included development of close military, economic, and political relations with Germany to be carried out with the help of Austrian Nazis. He also agreed to a reconstruction of the cabinet that would place Austrian Nazis in charge of some ministries. Seyss-Inquart secretly transmitted these concessions to Hitler.

Involved in major changes in the German military command structure and in the diplomatic corps, Hitler seized on a meeting with the Austrian chancellor as a chance to divert attention away from the turmoil within the German government. By forcing public concessions from Schuschnigg, Hitler would win a diplomatic victory that would offset the effects of the purge of the generals and diplomats.

In the shift of diplomatic assignments, Hitler recalled Papen from Vienna. When they conferred on February 5, Hitler ordered Papen to return to Vienna and make the necessary arrangements for Schuschnigg's visit, with a promise that the July 11 agreement would be reaffirmed without any additional political demands. Hoping to improve Austro-German relations through this meeting, Schuschnigg accepted the invitation.

On February 12, Schuschnigg arrived at Berchtesgaden accompanied only by the Austrian Foreign Minister, Guido Schmidt. To overawe the Austrians, Hitler had summoned General Keitel, General Walter von Reichenau, commander of the military district adjacent to Vienna, and General Hugo von Sperrle, who had commanded the Condor Legion in Spain. Schuschnigg had come to Berchtesgaden expecting a dignified discussion between two gentlemen, but he encountered a storm. Hitler accused him of hostility towards Germany: Austria should have left the League of Nations when Germany did, Hitler raved; instead of supporting Germany, Austria had committed high treason by remaining in the League. In his tirade, Hitler styled himself the greatest German in history and swore to fulfill his divine mission of resolving the Austrian question. If Schuschnigg should dare to oppose Hitler by ordering resistance, German troops would overrun Austrian defenses within half an hour. Neither Britain, France, nor Italy would intervene to thwart his plans; and he swore that he was not bluffing. Caught off guard by Hitler's assault, Schuschnigg apologized. Suddenly Hitler cut short his tirade for luncheon, which was accompanied by polite conversation about horses, motor cars, and such. Afterwards the host withdrew, leaving Schuschnigg and Austrian Foreign Minister Guido Schmidt alone with a few German generals who had been summoned there for the purpose of intimidating the Austrians.

While the victims waited, Hitler, Ribbentrop, and Papen prepared demands for further concessions based on those already granted earlier in Vienna. Then in mid-afternoon, they presented Schuschnigg with two typewritten pages containing the demands. Schuschnigg must promise to exchange views with Hitler on foreign policy and to assist Hitler's policies. The Austrian Nazi party could not be outlawed. Economic discrimination against Nazis in the government and armed forces, must be ended. Schuschnigg must appoint Seyss-Inquart Minister of the Interior with special authority to oversee the activities of the Austrian Nazis; the position would also give him supervision of the police. A general amnesty must be proclaimed for Austrian Nazis who had been imprisoned for breaking the law; people sympathetic to the Nazis must be given important positions in the Austrian Press Bureau. Better relations between the German and Austrian armies would be fostered by conferences between the General Staffs and by an exchange of officers; the Austrian Chief of Staff should be replaced by a general who would be friendly to Germany. If Schuschnigg carried out these demands, Austria would be well on the way to becoming a German satellite.

Stunned, Schuschnigg protested: he had been promised only affirmation of the July 11 agreement, not a new set of demands. After the failure of Ribbentrop and Papen to persuade the Austrian Chancellor, Hitler summoned Schuschnigg for a fresh attack. He demanded that Schuschnigg sign the document or Germany would take action that very night. Schuschnigg refused, claiming that he lacked authority to sign such a document. Hitler stepped hurriedly to the door.

"General Keitel!" he shouted.
"I shall have you called later," he yelled at Schuschnigg.[2]

Keitel, the new chief of the High Command, entered quickly and Schuschnigg left the room. Because of Hitler's threats, Schuschnigg imagined the worst—Hitler must be giving Keitel orders for an attack. Actually Hitler was only bluffing but the agonizing minutes that passed had the desired effect on Schuschnigg. Finally, when he reappeared, Hitler graciously offered to give Schuschnigg three days to accept the new demands. Confused, isolated, fearful of war, Schuschnigg gave in. When he returned to Vienna, Schuschnigg covered up the threat to Austrian independence because of rumors of German war preparations, which had been purposely instigated by Hitler shortly after Schuschnigg left Berchtesgaden. The French government, after learning a portion of the truth, expressed concern to Berlin and was in turn rebuffed. The British Foreign Office was helpless because of the struggle then going on between Eden and Chamberlain. Neither government wanted to go to war for the sake of Austria. Schuschnigg also sought advice from Mussolini, who recommended that he accept Hitler's demands. Forsaken by the Stresa powers, who had publicly sworn to uphold the independence of Austria, and determined to avoid the outbreak of war, Schuschnigg yielded on February 15.

From Hitler's references to Austria in the weeks following the Berchtesgaden meeting, it is clear that he expected the February demands to complete the July agreement and accomplish *Anschluss.* As a result of those most recent concessions, the Austrian Nazis became bolder, and the police—thanks to Seyss-Inquart, the new Minister of the Interior—became more undependable. After a few feeble efforts to arouse the nation, Schuschnigg finally decided to seek support by means of a national plebiscite to be held on March 13. He hoped a favorable vote would unite the nation behind him, but he had already gone too far in transforming Austria into a German satellite. One plebiscite could not arouse sufficient resistance to *Anschluss.* Guns, tanks, and soldiers, not votes, were required to withstand German aggression.

However, if the plebiscite succeeded, it would be an immense propaganda victory for Schuschnigg. Thanks to a spy in an Austrian cabinet ministry, Hitler learned of the plebiscite before Schuschnigg announced it publicly. Infuriated, Hitler intervened. He ordered the generals commanding troops in the areas along the Austrian frontier to report to him early on the morning of March 10, and asked to be given the plans for invasion of Austria. But Keitel had to confess that there was only the barest sketch of a proposed study for an invasion of Austria, and that only in case of an attempted restoration of the Habsburg monarchy. Because there were other more pressing projects, and because Hitler had emphasized Czechoslovakia first, very little consideration had been given to Austria. Hitler ordered that plans be prepared quickly for an invasion of Austria, presumably to establish constitutional conditions and protect the Germans within Austria.

It was decided that the Eighth Army would march into Austria while the Luftwaffe would drop propaganda leaflets, occupy airfields, and lend support to the army. The troops were ordered to appear reluctant in taking action against their Austrian brethren. They should avoid bloodshed to give the operation the appearance of friendly troops being welcomed by the population. However, any resistance should be crushed. Hitler wished to appear peaceful for two reasons. He hoped to avoid resistance from sentimental Austrians who might be seduced by an appeal to their cultural ties with Germany. Further, if the occupation could be brought off peacefully, it would seem to western Europe to be nothing more than a reunion of the German people who had suffered so badly from the flaws of the Versailles treaty.

In the midst of all of this, there was one unknown element—Mussolini. Because his forces were tied down by the Spanish Civil War, he could not have prevented the *Anschluss* had he been so inclined. But, unless Hitler were sure of what his response would be, there was the possibility that he might cause trouble. Consequently, Hitler dispatched Prince Philip of Hesse, the son-in-law of the King of Italy, to Mussolini with a letter that "revealed" an Austro-Czechoslovak plot against Germany. The plot, which was pure fabrication, detailed how both countries were strengthening their borders and preparing for a restoration of the Habsburgs, an event that might require an attack on Germany. Schuschnigg, according to the letter, had broken his promise by scheduling a plebiscite with the intent of oppressing the people and engulfing Austria in anarchy. "In my responsibility as Fuehrer and Chancellor of the German Reich and likewise as a son of this soil," he wrote to Mussolini, "I can no longer remain passive in the face of these developments."[3] Law and order had to be restored in Austria in order to defend Germany. Hitler promised not to overstep the boundary into Italy; he would stop short of the Brenner Pass, and those Germans below the pass who might want to join the Reich would have to have their wishes unfulfilled. When Mussolini replied that he had already written off Austria, an ecstatic Hitler swore, "I will never forget, whatever may happen. If he should ever need any help or be in any danger, he can be convinced that I shall stick by him, whatever may happen, even if the whole world were against him."[4]

By 4:30 A.M. on March 11, German frontier officials had closed the Austrian borders. Later in the day, two Austrian ministers acting for Hitler brought Schuschnigg an ultimatum: postpone the plebiscite and arrange for a new one that would be slanted

in favor of the Austrian Nazis or face armed German intervention. Arguments and conferences followed; and, in the afternoon, Schuschnigg called off the plebiscite, but Hitler would
not let it go at that. Within half an hour, Goering telephoned
an order for Schuschnigg and his government to resign. Seyss-
Inquart, Schuschnigg's "friend," should form a new government.
Schuschnigg was immediately ready to capitulate, but President
Wilhelm Miklas refused to accept the new chancellor and,
throughout the afternoon, searched for someone else to take
on the burden of leading Austria in this crucial period.

During the afternoon, Schuschnigg asked the advice of the
British government, but the reply was chilling: "His Majesty's
Government cannot take the responsibility of advising the Chancellor to take any course of action which might expose his country to dangers against which His Majesty's Government are
unable to guarantee protection."[5] Nor could France offer help.
The French cabinet had fallen on March 9; and now, as in the
Rhineland crisis, a caretaker government was in office. Both Paris
and London did make a halfhearted gesture toward consulting
Mussolini on the subject, but when he received their suggestion
rather coldly, they did not press the issue. Both governments
made routine protests to the German Foreign Ministry, but these
were simply for the record.

The attitude of the two western nations reinforced Schuschnigg's decision to resign. A peaceful surrender seemed the only
alternative to a short bloody war that, he was certain, would result
in the defeat of Austria. The Austrian forces could have delayed
the German advance for only a few days at most because they
had only about a two-day supply of ammunition, and the Austrian Nazis would have been certain to engage in rioting and
sabotage to divert troops. Austria was clearly outmatched—its
air force and anti-aircraft defenses were nonexistent, and its
artillery and tanks were few and old. Schuschnigg had no real
choice but to reject the advice of those who begged him to
attempt to block the German invasion. Had anyone cared,
Austrian resistance to the German invasion could have served
as a warning to Europe, but the nations of Europe did not judge
their vital interests to be at stake.

Late in the afternoon of March 11, Schuschnigg ordered the
Austrian troops to withdraw from the frontier and to offer no

resistance. Early in the evening, Schuschnigg's resignation was announced over the radio, and he went on the air later to announce that Austria would yield. In the streets of Vienna, the Nazis began to take control. Although German agents were already filtering into the Chancellery in Vienna, Seyss-Inquart had not yet become chancellor. About 8:45 P.M., Hitler decided it was necessary to launch the invasion. To give him a "legal" excuse for the invasion, it was necessary for Goering, who had been keeping in touch with Austrian Nazi agents in Vienna by telephone, to dictate a message to be wired to Berlin over Seyss-Inquart's signature calling for the entrance of German troops to prevent bloodshed and to restore law and order. The message was sent—after Hitler had ordered the invasion. In the early morning hours of March 12, Miklas gave in and Seyss-Inquart became chancellor. As his first task, he attempted unsuccessfully to halt the invasion.

When the German Eighth Army crossed into Austria later in the morning, it met no resistance, but progress was slow. Once across the Austrian border, the invading forces became snarled in traffic jams when vehicles broke down. Tanks had to be fueled at Austrian gasoline stations. One Panzer commander had to plan the invasion route using a Baedecker tourist guide to Austria. Nevertheless, in the afternoon, Hitler entered Austria and received a joyous welcome from the citizens of Linz where he had spent his boyhood.

It was there that he came to his decision that a puppet government headed by Seyss-Inquart was a less desirable alternative than *Anschluss.* Moreover, since occupation had been accomplished with no opposition and with only mild protestation from foreign governments, *Anschluss* could be achieved with little difficulty. During the crisis, Hitler had wavered in his opinion of foreign reaction. Later, in regard to Danzig and the Polish Corridor, he would be able to claim to be retaking German territory unjustly ripped away by the Treaty of Versailles. But this was not the case with Austria. Moreover, because the invasion of Austria meant going to the brink of war, Hitler had wavered, but his judgment of how Europe would react proved to be sound. The nations of Europe were just as relieved as Hitler when, on

March 13, in compliance with Hitler's decision, the puppet government in Austria adopted a law declaring the country to be a province of the German Reich. Hitler's victory was sealed with a plebiscite on April 10, when over 99 percent of the Austrian voters approved the question "Do you acknowledge Adolf Hitler as our Fuehrer and the reunion of Austria with the German Reich which was affected on March 11, 1938?" Many voted *ja* out of sheer relief that the uncertainty over Austria's future had ended.

The *Anschluss* was the greatest triumph that Hitler had experienced. Those in Germany who had doubted him had been proven wrong. The western powers had taken no action; they were unwilling to intervene. Hitler now felt that he could do whatever he wished to do. No one could oppose him either at home or abroad. No one could stand in his way. He had ignored anyone who advised moderation in his foreign policy. Now that he had brought Austria in the "Greater Germany," his next target was Czechoslovakia whose defenses had been weakened by the *Anschlus*.

However, this victory marked a change in Hitler's tactics. After this he would cease to concern himself simply with ending restrictions imposed on Germany by the Treaty of Versailles, and he would threaten independent nations with invasion, or even war, unless they capitulated to his demands. The results of his victory were impressive: without a shot being fired, without losing a soldier, and with only a few Austrian units mobilized, Germany had acquired $6^{1}/_{2}$ million new citizens who would provide additional labor and men for eight new army divisions. In addition, Germany obtained Austrian reserves of hard currency which would help supply the raw material and foreign exchange needs of Germany. The balance of power in Central Europe had been upset. With Germany now surrounding Czechoslovakia on three fronts, the Czechoslovak defenses were outflanked; and Yugoslavia, Italy, and Hungary were now confronted with German troops on their frontiers. Without the guns of the Wehrmacht being fired, one of the states that had emerged from the 1919 peace settlement had surrendered to German armies. Hitler had won his first conquest in World War II.

CRISIS IN CZECHOSLOVAKIA

The successful *Anschluss* of Germany and Austria directly threatened the security of Czechoslovakia, whose defenses along the Austrian frontier had been allowed to weaken. Because the interests of Czechoslovakia were affected by the *Anschluss*, German officials took pains to inform the Prague government that the affair concerned only Germany and Austria and that Czechoslovakia should not be alarmed. But there was cause for alarm. Czechoslovakia contained the Sudeten Germans, a minority with dissatisfactions that could be exploited by Hitler to weaken the security of the country. Although Hitler actually had no interest in the grievances of the Sudeten Germans, he saw that they might be used to his advantage.

Moreover, if grievances were lacking, they would be created. The Sudeten Germans would be led to believe that Nazi Germany had a deep interest in their safety and welfare. In this way they would become the cause for an attack on Czechoslovakia. Germany would appear as the protector of the Sudeten Germans. When needed, incidents would be provoked to start the war. If necessary, they would be manufactured.

Scattered along the western frontiers of Czechoslovakia—in Bohemia and Moravia—were a large number of people whose ancestors had migrated from Germany. Although some had come as early as the twelfth century, they still considered themselves German in origin and culture. In the eighteenth century, at the invitation of the Austrian monarchy, a second wave of migrants followed, helping make the Sudetens the dominant political force in Bohemia and Moravia. The territory of these two provinces had never belonged to Germany (although they had at one time been a part of Austria-Hungary), and no one had driven the emigrants to leave their German homeland. They had migrated of their own free will. But the ancestral loyalties of this displaced people were to create difficulties for their adopted home.

When the borders of the new state of Czechoslovakia were under discussion at the Paris peace conference, the Sudeten Germans attempted to have the territory joined to Austria or Germany, but these efforts were blocked by the French delega-

tion, which argued for keeping the Sudetenland within Czechoslovakia so that the new state would be large enough to block
Germany on the east. Consequently, the ancient southeastern
border of Germany remained unchanged except for slight al-
terations.

But the Sudetens resented the decisions of the conference,
and refused to cooperate with the new Czechoslovak government until 1926, when they realized they could expect no help
from Berlin. To further complicate the situation, they had
become embittered by the depression, and they blamed the
economic situation on their government. Therefore, when the
Nazis came to power in Germany, they had no difficulty in re-
vitalizing the Sudeten German party, a small Nazi organization
led by Konrad Henlein. Subsidized by Berlin, the party agitated
for Sudeten autonomy, a policy that would be harmful to Czechoslovak security because the Sudetenland contained important
fortifications against Germany. However, the demand for autonomy concealed Henlein's real goal, which was the eventual
inclusion of Bohemia and Moravia within the German Reich.
Once the area had been incorporated within Germany, then the
rest of Czechoslovakia would be defenseless against Hitler's
armies.

On March 28, 1938, Hitler personally instructed Henlein to
make such outrageous demands of the government that it would
be impossible to meet them. In return for Henlein's assistance,
Hitler pledged full personal support for his new "viceroy." Speaking for Hitler, Ribbentrop emphasized to Henlein the next day
that the Sudeten German party must not expect to be more than
a front for the Reich, but that it must present itself as the leader
in the campaign of the German minority to achieve complete
autonomy. Whatever enticement the Czechs might offer, Henlein
must not accept an invitation to join the Czechoslovak government. Henlein and the Sudeten German party must endeavor
to make their subversion appear to be simply a minority seeking self-determination in the face of alleged persecution, thereby
arousing the sympathies of countries already troubled by the
Versailles treaty.

At the Sudeten Party Congress in Karlsbad on April 24,
Henlein, following instructions, called for a series of changes

in the government of the Sudetenland. He wanted the Sudetens recognized as a "legal entity," with an autonomous government staffed by Sudeten officials; and those Sudetens who lived outside the autonomous areas must be provided with legal protection. He insisted that Sudetens were to be compensated for all the financial losses suffered at the hands of the government since 1918. Finally, the Sudetens should be permitted complete freedom to profess a German ideology—nazism.

If the government were to grant these demands, the result would be a Nazi state within the boundaries of Czechoslovakia and very near the German border. But Henlein did not intend for the Karlsbad demands to be fulfilled; he meant only to harass the Czechoslovak government, to hamper its relations with Britain and France, and to create the impression that the Sudetenland had been torn from Germany by the Treaty of Versailles.

The relations of Czechoslovakia with Britain and France were the special concern of Eduard Benes, the president of Czechoslovakia. Benes had, with Thomas Masaryk, been one of the founders of the new state, and distinguished himself in international affairs as the first Czechoslovak Foreign Minister. He had negotiated a treaty of mutual assistance with France as a corollary to the Locarno Pact wherein both nations promised to come to the aid of the other in case of unprovoked attack; and he was also responsible for a treaty with the Soviet Union pledging aid to each other if one were attacked without provocation, but with the provision that France must first come to the aid of the victim. Benes thought that these treaties were sufficient to protect Czechoslovakia.

He had no difficulty in recognizing the dangers in Henlein's program: not only would it damage the Czech defenses, but it would also create a dangerous precedent, prompting other minorities to demand similar privileges and further weakening the already precarious national unity. With many autonomous groups competing for national rights, the nation might easily fall apart. To preserve Czechoslovakia as a political entity, Benes bargained and negotiated to try to restrict Sudeten demands.

However, in London and Paris, those who sought to appease Hitler regarded the efforts of Benes as dangerous to peace. To Neville Chamberlain, Czechoslovakia was a threat to the peace as long as the Sudetenland was an object of dispute. It was not simply that Chamberlain feared an invasion of Czechoslovakia by Hitler's armies, although this was one of his considerations. But under the influence of German propaganda, he also considered the Sudeten complaints of Czech discrimination to be wholly just. Chamberlain was certain that the only way to prevent German armies from overrunning Czechoslovakia was to settle the Sudeten German question on terms satisfactory to Hitler. The Prime Minister believed that, should there be a war over this area, any peace settlement would be forced to give the Sudetenland to Germany simply to prevent future clashes.

Moreover, Chamberlain would not commit Britain to Czechoslovakia except as specified by the Covenant of the League of Nations, which called upon the members of the League to protect the territorial integrity and independence of every member of the League of Nations against aggression. On March 24, 1938, he explained to the House of Commons that these obligations would not, without careful consideration, be interpreted in any way that would endanger British interests. If because of the Locarno Pact, France became involved in war with Germany, Chamberlain was willing only to imply that Britain might be drawn into the conflict. By avoiding a precise warning, he hoped to be able to deter any German action against France without having to resort to fighting.

Any chance that the Chamberlain government would take a firm stand against German aggression was weakened by a report from the British Chiefs of Staff, dated March 28, 1938, in response to a request by Chamberlain to report on the military implications of German aggression against Czechoslovakia. The Chiefs concluded that there was no pressure that Britain and any possible allies could bring to bear that could prevent Germany from overrunning Bohemia and defeating the Czechoslovak army. Britain would be forced to undertake a war against Germany to restore Czechoslovakia that would likely become a world war involving Italy and Japan. Regardless of any possible aid from allies, the Chiefs could not anticipate when Britain would be strong enough to withstand Germany, Italy, and Japan simultaneously.

Whatever policy Britain should choose would greatly concern France, particularly the new government headed by Premier

Edouard Daladier and Foreign Minister Georges Bonnet. Although Daladier was well aware of Hitler's drive to dominate Europe, he had no wish to support Czechoslovakia if it meant a war with Germany. As for Bonnet, he believed that a war over Czechoslovakia would be a worse disaster for France than the Franco-Prussian War had been. Bonnet preferred any sacrifice to avoid a war with Germany.

On March 15, before becoming premier, Daladier as Minister of Defense had informed the Permanent Committee on National Defense that France could not give Czechoslovakia direct aid. France could only mobilize troops and hold German soldiers on the frontier. Neither Daladier nor General Maurice Gamelin, Army Chief of Staff, made any preparations to come to the defense of Czechoslovakia, which they considered a hopeless cause.

On April 28–29, when Daladier and Bonnet conferred with Chamberlain and Halifax in London, they put on a bold front in an effort to trick the British into believing that France would go to war on behalf of Czechoslovakia. But Daladier, who offered no plan to aid Czechoslovakia, could only suggest that if Britain and France made clear their determination to maintain the peace of Europe through respect for the liberties and rights of independent peoples, war would be avoided. Chamberlain lamented British military unpreparedness and told Daladier that he could expect only two underequipped divisions if there should be war with Germany. Reluctantly, he agreed to staff discussions on air and naval assistance. Although Daladier continually warned him against Hitler, Chamberlain could not believe Hitler wanted to destroy Czechoslovakia. Because his Chiefs of Staff had indicated that Czechoslovakia could be saved only by a full-scale war, the Prime Minister was unwilling to attempt to bluff the Fuehrer, unlike Daladier. Instead, Chamberlain insisted that the Czechoslovak government must accept Henlein's demands. Because Daladier and Bonnet had no intention of acting independently of the British government, they were delighted to have Britain take the lead in forcing Czechoslovakia to make concessions.

Next London assured the German Foreign Minister that Prague would be instructed to seek a settlement through direct negotiations with the Sudeten Germans. Prague soon learned that it would have support neither from Britain nor France so long as it opposed the Sudeten demands. Negotiations must continue until a comprehensive settlement could be reached, one that would encompass all of the Sudeten demands. But Hitler had no intention of permitting an agreement to be concluded between the Sudeten German party and the Prague government settling Sudeten German demands. He wanted a war.

However, before negotiations could begin, a new crisis erupted: on May 19, without explanation, Henlein left the country for Austria. The Czechoslovak government had no way of knowing how to interpret his action. Was he on his way to Hitler to receive the orders that would bring on a coup? Rumors were circulating about German troop movements and Luftwaffe reconnaissance flights near the Czechoslovak frontier. Torrents of abuse against the Czech nation poured from the Nazi presses. Late on May 20, the frightened Prague cabinet called up reservists, who continued to move to their posts late into the night, expecting German bombers at any moment. When dawn came, the Czech troops were at their posts, but there had been no German attack.

As a result of the rumors and the seemingly imminent German attack, the British government announced with some reluctance that, if a conflict should occur and France should intervene, Britain could become involved. In Paris, Bonnet was terrified that the Czech mobilization might provoke Hitler into action. Once aroused, Hitler could be expected to turn on Paris, which, it was feared, "would be destroyed meter by meter through German air attacks."[6] Nevertheless, Bonnet did announce that France would stand behind its pledge to give military assistance to Czechoslovakia, but he hoped that "Germany would do nothing to put France in the position where her treaty obligations would oblige her to intervene."[7]

When German officials denied that they were preparing an invasion, they were telling the truth. There was an increase in military traffic, but this was apparently due to the integration of Austrian army units into the Wehrmacht combined with the usual movement of troops on regular training maneuvers. There is also the possibility that some German troops were directed eastward to test the Czech reaction. As for Hitler, he was hard at work (unusual for him) on plans for the war against Czechoslovakia.

By May 23, when Henlein returned from Germany, the crisis had died down, but its effects lingered. London and Paris exerted greater pressure on the Czechs to grant concessions to the Sudeten Germans. To Berlin, the crisis revealed the Czechoslovak determination to fight. For Prague, the events of May had the effect of giving the Czechoslovak army the opportunity to practice mobilization.

Actually, on April 21, Hitler had discussed his plan for the invasion of Czechoslovakia—known as *Operation Green*—with Keitel; and a preliminary directive had been started, but it was unfinished at the time of the crisis of May 20. On May 28, to an audience consisting of Goering, Ribbentrop, Neurath, General Ludwig Beck, Keitel, Brauchitsch, and Raeder, Hitler announced: "It is my unshakeable will that Czechoslovakia shall disappear from the map."[8] The problem of living space had to be solved quickly. Should Germany attempt to acquire this needed *Lebensraum*, however, Hitler was certain that they would face opposition from Britain and France. In anticipation of a war against the nations of western Europe, Germany must first get rid of the threat to the east—Czechoslovakia. Since it was apparent that Britain and France wanted to avoid war, and since no other powers would oppose Germany, Hitler ordered his generals to complete the fortifications facing France and to conclude the plans for the invasion of Czechoslovakia before Britain and France rearmed and while they were still involved with Italy over the Spanish Civil War. The time had come for Hitler to have the first of his short wars.

On May 30, Hitler signed a directive for an invasion of Czechoslovakia to be launched no later than October 1, 1938. It was his intention to "smash Czechoslovakia by military action in the near future,"[9] utilizing whatever opportunity might offer the best chance for success. He ordered immediate preparations to exploit any incident that would offer a valid excuse for war. They must use surprise and speed in wiping out the Czechoslovak forces to present western Europe with a fait accompli. In order to achieve this swift conquest of Czechoslovakia and to make any Anglo-French intervention pointless, all of the might of the Wehrmacht would have to be turned on Czechoslovakia, with only a screening force for the western border. When the hopelessness of the Czechoslovak cause had become apparent, Hitler expected other nations, chiefly Poland and Hungary, which had territorial claims on Czechoslovakia, to intervene. If Britain and France did intervene, Operation Green would have to be continued until there was nothing left of Czechoslovakia, then all of the Wehrmacht would be turned on the West.

Although Hitler still intended to exploit whatever opportunity that developed, the May 30 directive omitted all references to freeing the "oppressed" Sudeten Germans. The omission was not accidental; Hitler had merely used the Sudetens to conceal his goal: a planned attack on Czechoslovakia.

As spring became summer, reports, threats, and rumors of German war preparations magnified French fears that Germany might suddenly attack Czechoslovakia and confront France with a decision of war or peace. The French ambassador in Germany reported that Hitler nourished the ambition to celebrate the end of the Treaty of Versailles in the Hall of Mirrors in the Palace of Versailles. There were reports that German fortifications on the western frontier were being rushed to completion.

The reports and rumors about German war preparations so terrified Bonnet that on July 20 he called in the Czechoslovak minister and announced that France would not go to war over the Sudeten affair. "In no case should the Czechoslovak government believe that if war breaks out we will be at its side. . . . The Czechoslovak government must be convinced that neither France nor England will go to War."[10] The French minister in Prague informed Benes, who begged that this matter remain top secret. Bonnet was only too happy to comply and thus maintain publicly the fiction that France would fight for Czechoslovakia.

Throughout that summer, the Czechoslovak government had great difficulty with the Sudeten negotiators. Whatever Prague proposed, the Sudetens always found an excuse to reject. From Berlin, the Nazi press hurled threats at the people of Czechoslovakia, and from London and Paris came pleas for immediate concessions to all the Sudeten demands—although both governments knew very well that German military preparations were underway and that a German attack on Czechoslovakia was planned for the autumn.

To hasten a settlement before there could be a war, Chamberlain and Halifax adopted a new method: they dispatched a mediator to Czechoslovakia to bring both parties to agreement. Walter Runciman, a millionaire shipbuilder without any experience in European minority problems, was chosen to undertake this task. Chamberlain publicly announced that Runciman would be acting only in a personal capacity, but the truth was that he was an official agent of the British government, and he had been instructed to force Benes to accept a solution that would be pleasing to the Sudeten Germans and to Hitler.

Chamberlain and Halifax had blackmailed Benes into accepting Runciman as a mediator, threatening that, if he should refuse, they would leak the fact to the newspapers. Then the Czechoslovak government would stand condemned for turning down peaceful mediation. But Hitler had no wish for peaceful mediation of the crisis.

Runciman reached Prague early in August, and immediately he was inundated by a mountain of Sudeten memoranda, articles, and documents that were intended to convince him that the problem could not be solved under the existing circumstances. Runciman aggravated matters by spending his weekends in the homes of wealthy Sudetens, who filled his ears with stories of their suffering countrymen. He came to believe these tales and endeavored to force Benes into granting all of the Sudeten demands. At last Benes realized that, if he wanted to hold the sympathy of Britain and France, he had no alternative but to give in.

Early in September, to pacify London and Paris, the Czechoslovak cabinet offered the Sudeten leaders most of the Karlsbad demands. Suddenly the Sudetens were faced with the awful prospect of accepting the cabinet's proposals or risking exposure of their plot. Worst of all, Hitler could be deprived of his war. However, they were rescued from this dilemma by a "riot" in a Czech town. On September 7, when a group of Sudeten deputies visited fellow party members who had been imprisoned for gun-running, a street brawl staged by the Sudeten Germans erupted, which soon attracted curious Czechs. In the process of ending the brawl, the police managed to rough up some of the deputies, giving the Sudetens the excuse of police brutality to halt the negotiations. The government moved quickly to make amends by firing the policemen involved, and the negotiations were scheduled to resume on September 13.

However, on September 12, in a speech broadcast to the world, Hitler denounced the Czechoslovak government for its treatment of the Sudeten minority:

> The misery of the Sudeten Germans is indescribable. It is sought to annihilate them. As human beings they are oppressed and scandalously treated in an intolerable fashion. When three and a half million members of a people which numbers nearly eighty million may not sing a song they like simply because it does not please the Czechs, or when they are beaten until the blood flows solely because they wear stockings the sight of which offends the Czechs, or when they are terrorized and ill-treated because they use a form of greeting which the Czechs dislike, . . . when they are hunted and harried like helpless wild fowl for every expression of national sentiment—this may perhaps cause the worthy representatives of our democracies no concern: they may possibly welcome it since in this case only some three and a half million Germans are in question; but I can only say to the representatives of these democracies that this does concern us, and that if these tortured creatures can of themselves find no justice and no help they will get both from us. The depriving of these people of their rights must come to an end.[11]

Before this tirade ended, the riots had exploded into civil war in the Sudentenland, forcing Prague to dispatch troops. Again, the Sudenten leaders broke off negotiations. Henlein fled across the frontier; and, from the safety of Germany, he issued a proclamation calling for the "return" of the Sudentenland to the German Reich. At last, they had been able to give the world the impression that Germany had a right to the Sudentenland, and Hitler would be able to press for the direct inclusion of the territory within the German nation.

When the news of the fighting in the Sudentenland reached Paris, there was panic. Daladier begged Chamberlain to do whatever he could to prevent German troops from entering Czechoslovakia, otherwise France would be obliged to fulfill its promise to aid Czechoslovakia. By this plea, Daladier in effect delivered French foreign policy into the hands of the British Prime Minister. For some time Chamberlain had been considering a personal meeting with Hitler, and now, without consulting either the British, French, or Czechoslovak cabinets, he requested an invitation from Hitler to visit Germany and confer with him. Astonished by Chamberlain's request, Hitler had to extend an invitation for this unexpected meeting; and in search of peace, the British politician embarked on his first airplane ride.

Hitler and Chamberlain met on September 15 at Berchtesgaden. After a pleasant tea, they held their conference—in the same room where Schuschnigg and Hitler had met in February. Hitler threatened war if the Sudetenland were not given to the Reich. If Hitler was so determined on war, Chamberlain indicated that he might as well return to London. Realizing that he had gone too far, Hitler proposed that the Sudetenland could be ceded to Germany on the basis of self-determination, in line with Chamberlain's thinking. Mollified, Chamberlain promised to do what he could to give Hitler what he wanted. For his part, Hitler promised Chamberlain not to give the order for war during the next few days. In truth, his timetable did not call for war for at least two weeks. Chamberlain left Berchtesgaden believing that he had prevented the outbreak of world war.

When Chamberlain returned to London, he encountered no opposition from the cabinet. He informed them that he believed that Hitler was truthful when he had said that he wanted the Sudeten problem solved. Chamberlain thought that Hitler's objectives were strictly limited and that Hitler could be relied upon after giving his word. No one in the cabinet gave Chamberlain any trouble. The cabinet even discussed a possible guarantee of Czechoslovakia's new frontiers.

While the British cabinet debated, Hitler took steps to ensure that war would come as soon as military preparations were completed by establishing the Sudeten German Free Corps to launch terrorist attacks along the German-Czechoslovak frontier. These gangs of thugs were to create incidents which would supply Hitler with the pretext for war with Czechoslovakia. As an added precaution in case the Prague government accepted all of his demands, Hitler prodded the Polish and Hungarian governments to demand concessions from the Czechs for their minorities.

On September 18 and 19, Daladier and Bonnet came to London for a conference with Chamberlain and Halifax. When confronted with the Hitler-Chamberlain solution, Daladier rejected the use of self-determination through a plebiscite lest it open up all of Central Europe to Hitler. But Daladier's generals had warned him before he left Paris that Germany possessed the strength to crush Czechoslovakia in only a few days. With this in mind, he accepted Chamberlain's proposal. To satisfy the French, Chamberlain promised to guarantee the new Czechoslovakia. Here was a genuine revolution in British foreign policy: Chamberlain had promised that Britain would guarantee a frontier deep in Central Europe, far from the English Channel. Nothing comparable had occurred since the agreement with Frederick the Great in 1756 to guarantee Prussia.

Benes and his cabinet rejected the Anglo-French proposal and insisted upon arbitration of the matter. But London and Paris changed their proposal to an ultimatum: unless Czechoslovakia accepted the proposal, Chamberlain would cease his efforts to avert war and France would refuse aid to Czechoslovakia if war broke out. On September 21, the Czechoslovak cabinet capitulated: and, on September 22, Chamberlain met Hitler again, this time at Godesberg. Believing that he had saved Europe from war, the Prime Minister reported to Hitler as a chairman of the board would address an annual stockholders meeting. He was certainly not prepared for the response he was to receive from Hitler. The report was unacceptable to the Fuehrer. The injustices suffered by all the minorities in Czechoslovakia had to be redressed. There were Polish and Hungarian demands that had already arisen and must be settled if peace were to be established in Central Europe. Speed was essential because of the disorder in the frontier areas (created by the Free Corps as ordered by Hitler). The frontier between Germany and Czechoslovakia must be redrawn immediately and must be based on language. Czechoslovak soldiers must be withdrawn from the new German territory at once, and a German occupation force must be allowed into the ceded area. Chamberlain wanted—and thought he had

Nazi Aggression in Central Europe, 1933–1939

effected—a more leisurely takeover. The Fuehrer and the Prime Minister exchanged angry words, and the meeting ended in deadlock.

The next day Hitler sent Chamberlain a memorandum spelling out his demands. The evacuation of the Sudetenland would commence on September 26 and be over by the 28th. The entire area must be handed over to the Germans without damage to property or installations; nothing could be evacuated except people. A map attached to the memorandum indicated the areas that the German troops would occupy; in effect, Germany would be occupying sufficient area to cripple Czechoslovak defenses.

Hitler's demands were intended to block a peaceful solution to Sudeten German problem.

Meeting again with Hitler in the evening of September 23, Chamberlain again objected to Hitler's demand for immediate occupation, but the Fuehrer insisted on a speedy solution to a problem that had been left unsolved for twenty years. Chamberlain complained about Hitler's memorandum sounding so much like an ultimatum. And the occupation of areas that were not ethnically German disturbed him. Hitler spurned Chamberlain's complaints and made only one concession: the Czech evacuation did not have to begin until October 1—the final date he had considered for *Operation Green.*

On September 24, before the conference ended, the Czechs had mobilized their armed forces and refused the Godesberg demands. At first, the French cabinet reluctantly agreed to stand by their ally; but, in a conference with Chamberlain, Halifax, Simon, and Hoare in London on September 25 and 26, Daladier and Bonnet were unable to come up with joint war plans. Instead, the English occupied the meeting with interrogating the French about their plans and preparations and trying to pressure them to abandon Czechoslovakia to Hitler. Only after he was convinced that Daladier was determined to support Czechoslovakia did Chamberlain promise British aid to France, but he made no pledge of direct help to Czechoslovakia. If France should decide not to fight, then Britain had no obligation.

On September 26, Chamberlain dispatched Sir Horace Wilson, his special advisor, to Hitler to convey the results of the Anglo-French meeting. Wilson was unable, in his two violent interviews with Hitler, to receive any significant response from the Fuehrer. Instead of responding, Hitler raved incoherently about Britain and France attacking Germany because the Czechs had precipitated a war by rejecting his demands. In a speech in the Sportpalast on September 26, Hitler implied that war was near unless the Sudetens were permitted to rejoin Germany; but in his official answer to Chamberlain, which arrived in London by letter on September 27, he promised to guarantee the integrity of the remainder of Czechoslovakia as well as to guarantee favorable treatment for Czechs remaining in the German-occupied territory. However, he continued to insist upon immediate occupation to halt the Czech delaying tactics. The final frontiers could always be straightened out later by plebiscite and negotiation.

The conciliatory tone of the letter implied that Hitler had changed, but he had written it simply for publication, as was evidenced by his quick permission to London to publish the letter. It is probable that the letter was drafted to avoid the kind of propaganda defeat Germany had received in 1914, when the ultimatums to Russia, France, and Belgium, followed by declarations of war, had given Germany the onus of aggressor.

Nevertheless, Europe braced itself for what was expected to come. In London and Paris, art collections were stowed away while trenches were dug in parks, gas masks were distributed to the public, anti-aircraft batteries were set up, and children were evacuated to the country. Prague ordered a blackout. And, in Berlin, Hitler ordered the first assault units to attack at 6:15 A.M. on September 30.

But the concern was not limited merely to France, Britain, and Czechoslovakia. In the United States, Franklin D. Roosevelt twice asked that talks resume, pointing out that the negotiators had already reached the most difficult hurdle of agreement in principle. Nor were the demands being made entirely by Germany. Polish Foreign Minister Jozef Beck demanded that Czechoslovakia immediately cede Teschen to Poland, and Hungary grew bold enough to request equal treatment for the Magyars living within Czechoslovakia. Although the Soviet Union would not become involved in a German-Czechoslovak conflict unless France should aid Czechoslovakia first, Soviet Commissar for Foreign Affairs Maxim Litvinov managed a threat to denounce the Soviet nonaggression pact with Poland if Polish troops should cross the Czechoslovak frontier. However, the Poles were not impressed.

But Chamberlain continued to labor for peace. Late on September 27, he appealed to Hitler with a new plan, providing for occupation of the Sudetenland according to a timetable. That night, he spoke to the nation in a radio broadcast:

> How horrible, fantastic, incredible it is that we should be digging trenches and trying on gas masks here because of a quarrel in a far-away country between people of whom we know

nothing. It seems still more impossible that a quarrel which has already been settled in principle should be the subject of war. . . . However much we may sympathize with a small nation confronted by a big, powerful neighbor, we cannot in all circumstances undertake to involve the whole British Empire in a war simply on her account. If we have to fight, it must be on larger issues than that.[12]

He followed this with another message to Hitler dispatched on the morning of September 28, announcing that he was prepared to come to Berlin to negotiate with Czechoslovak, Italian, and French representatives, promising that Britain and France would force Czechoslovakia to abide by the decisions of the conference. To reinforce this suggestion, Chamberlain had the British ambassador in Rome appeal to Mussolini to use his influence with Hitler. Frightened by the possibility of a war for which Italy was unprepared, Mussolini begged Hitler to accept the conference. The French ambassador in Berlin reinforced the new move by presenting a plan drafted by Bonnet calling for German troops to occupy important sections of the Sudetenland no later than October 1; France also promised to compel Czechoslovakia to fall into line.

With three capitals courting Hitler and promising so much to satisfy his demands, war would have been hard to justify. Hitler had been trapped by his own rhetoric because he had demanded self determination for the Sudeten Germans and it had been offered. By September 28, no nation—not even Czechoslovakia—continued to dispute Hitler's claims to the Sudetenland; the only disagreement was over the way the territory was to change hands. Britain and France had now offered him a blank check; the Soviet Union had indicated it would not intervene; and Poland, eager to get in on the spoils, offered no opposition.

If Hitler opted for war, the element of surprise had vanished. The French army was mobilizing, as had the British fleet and the Czechoslovak forces. At the same time, Hitler had observed an obvious lack of enthusiasm for war among the German people. Even among his advisors and generals, there were signs of reluctance to go to war. Under these conditions, Hitler could not insist on war, so he accepted the proposal for a high-level conference, provided Mussolini could come. The Duce accepted joyfully because he had no interest in going to war on behalf of the Sudeten Germans. Consequently, on the afternoon of September 28, invitations from Berlin for a summit conference to be held at Munich were dispatched to Daladier and Chamberlain—but no invitation was sent to Prague.

Chamberlain received the message about the conference while he was detailing the story of the summer's negotiations to the House of Commons: "I have now been informed by Herr Hitler that he invites me to meet him at Munich tomorrow morning. He has also invited Signor Mussolini and M. Daladier. Signor Mussolini has accepted and I have no doubt M. Daladier will also accept. I need not say what my answer will be."[13] The members broke into cheers, with only a handful keeping silent.

Besides the obvious reason for Hitler's acceptance of the conference, there were several pressures on him that were not so apparent. Some of his generals had expressed great concern over weaknesses in the western defenses, and Army Chief of Staff General Ludwig Beck had resigned in protest against Hitler's provoking a European war when he believed that Germany was unprepared. There is also the possibility that Chamberlain's promise to support France may have shaken Hitler's confidence that Britain was going to avoid war at all costs.

A few conspirators had communicated with London, begging Chamberlain to stand firm, call Hitler's bluff, and if necessary begin the war. Then the German generals would overthrow Hitler. Chamberlain rejected this plea because the past conduct of the German officer corps did not warrant trusting them in 1938. Had Chamberlain called Hitler's bluff and war broken out, the plot would surely have failed. Obscure German politicians and some conservative officers could never have aroused soldiers already converted to nazism to overthrow their popular Fuehrer in the midst of a war. The stench of treason would have been too strong.

Was Hitler bluffing? Did he accept the Munich Conference because Chamberlain called his bluff? Most of his contemporaries believed he was determined on war, not bluffing. Actually, it would be impossible to ascertain, because his bluff was never called. Too many wanted to avoid doing that, and when it was called finally in September 1939, war did come.

Certainly, Hitler had accepted the conference knowing that he would be able to dominate the meetings, overawe Daladier and Chamberlain, and win a personal victory. After all, his claims had been guaranteed in advance; war had become unnecessary unless he sought it himself. But Hitler's goal had been war, not a high-level meeting. Chamberlain had maneuvered him into calling the Munich Conference.

THE MUNICH CONFERENCE

About noon on September 29, the conference opened at Munich in the Fuehrerhaus. All of the principles at the meeting agreed with Hitler's insistence on speed; but, without a chairman and an agenda, the discussion wandered from topic to topic. Finally, Mussolini presented a memorandum that had been drafted in the German Foreign Ministry and had been handed to him before the conference opened. Because Chamberlain and Daladier had nothing to offer, this memorandum became the basis for discussion. The proceedings became extremely legalistic, with Chamberlain efficiently inquiring about such technical details as the relocation of cattle. With this, Hitler soon became unhappy because it limited his opportunities for frightening Daladier and Chamberlain. But Mussolini bustled about, enjoying the conference, thinking that he had been responsible for averting war.

Because no one kept out the uninvited, the conference room came to resemble a railroad station during a holiday weekend. At no time during the conference did Chamberlain and Daladier confer privately, although they did have the opportunity during a recess; and, late in the evening, the final drafts of the agreement were prepared. Early in the morning of September 30, the agreement was signed by the four heads of government.

The contents of the Munich Agreement called for the evacuation of Czechoslovak forces from an area that was designated on an attached map, beginning on October 1 and reaching completion by October 10. At the same time, in four stages, German troops would occupy the area. Conditions for the evacuation and occupation would be decided by an international commission with representatives from the four signatory powers plus Czechoslovakia. This commission would not only determine any additional areas to be occupied but also administer plebiscites and draw the final frontier. The British and French governments promised to guarantee the new frontiers against unprovoked aggression, but Italy and Germany would guarantee the new frontiers only after Hungarian and Polish claims had been satisfied. Czech compliance with the terms was mandatory.

Under the terms of the Munich Agreement, an independent nation lost vital territory containing important fortifications without a battle being fought. It was comparable only to the partition of Poland in the eighteenth century. At the Paris Peace Conference and after a long war, Germany had been permitted to submit objections to the terms of the Versailles treaty in writing; but, in 1938, even this was denied Czechoslovakia. The Czech representatives who came to Munich were simply summoned before Chamberlain and Daladier and informed that Czechoslovakia was considered to have already accepted the Munich Agreement and that there would be no appeal from this decision.

In the early morning hours of September 30, at his own request, Chamberlain met privately with Hitler without informing Daladier. The Prime Minister produced a statement on Anglo-German relations, carefully typed in duplicate, which he asked Hitler to sign. According to the statement, Hitler and Chamberlain regarded the Munich Agreement and the Anglo-German Naval Agreement as "symbolic of the desire of our two peoples never to go to war with one another again." In the future, "consultations" would be used to handle questions concerning Britain and Germany. They resolved to "continue our efforts to remove possible sources of difference and thus to contribute to assure the peace of Europe."[14] Hitler, tired and sleepy, signed the agreement without fully realizing what the elderly prime minister had done.

Chamberlain had managed to obtain Hitler's written promise to meet with him before making further territorial claims. It had been agreed that, henceforth, Anglo-German diplomacy would be conducted face-to-face by these two men. Together they would insure the peace of Europe. The efficient Prime Minister was confident: he expected Hitler to consult him as would any businessman who had signed a contract. But, although he had managed to obtain this small diplomatic victory, he had not secured "peace in our time," for Hitler did not view the sanctity of contracts in quite the same way as Chamberlain. He considered the statement as simply another indication that Britain would not block his plans in eastern Europe.

Shortly after noon on September 30, the Czechoslovak government formally accepted the agreement. The betrayed Czechoslovak people wept openly in the streets of Prague, while their soldiers began withdrawing from positions they had lost without a battle. Some of the generals did want to fight, but Benes ordered the withdrawal because the only alternative was a war fought alone against Germany, Poland, and possibly Hungary, and the Czechoslovak government would have been condemned for starting the war. A week after the Munich Conference, Benes resigned under German pressure and soon left Czechoslovakia.

Chamberlain and Daladier returned to their capitals to be lauded for their labors in behalf of peace. They were showered with gifts, and honors—such as streets being named for them—were heaped upon them. It was a time of rejoicing for the appeasers. However, Daladier was able to see the damage that had been done to European security, although he kept silent for political reasons. France had suffered a grievous defeat, and he realized that its position as a major European power was gone.

Although Chamberlain eventually was able to comprehend something of the enormity of the diplomatic defeat suffered at Munich, he was never really able to understand Hitler or the strategic importance of Czechoslovakia. He saw the crisis as "a quarrel in a faraway country between people of whom we know nothing."[15] His critics had wanted Chamberlain to call Hitler's bluff, but that was not Chamberlain's way of doing things. Perhaps more important, he knew that Britain was unprepared, both psychologically and militarily, for a war against Germany that would escalate into a world war; and he knew that, if he attempted to bluff Hitler, there would certainly have been a war. Chamberlain could not see the Sudetenland as a valid reason for the slaughter of millions, especially since the Sudetens wanted to be German anyway. Furthermore, he had confidence that, once this question was settled, Hitler would have no more territorial demands. Chamberlain's decision was also influenced by the opinions of the governments of the dominions, which were united in their opposition to war. The high commissioners of Australia, New Zealand, Canada, and South Africa pressured Chamberlain to accept Hitler's Godesberg demands.

At the time of the Munich crisis, Britain faced a concurrent crisis in the eastern Mediterranean which placed an intolerable strain on the nation's capabilities because full-scale rebellion had broken out in Palestine. By the end of the summer there was a call for a full division to be dispatched to Palestine to crush the revolt. However, to create this division, units would have to be collected from India, Egypt and Britain.

In an analysis, dated September 14, the Chiefs of Staff argued that the disposition of British forces must take into consideration the worst contingency. An intervention by Italy would create a crisis for Britain and France. If Japan were to take advantage of this situation, Britain might be forced to evacuate the Mediterranean and order the fleet to Singapore. The first commitment of British forces, after ensuring the safety of the United Kingdom, should be the security of Egypt and the interests in the Middle East. However, it might be essential to send a field force to France. There were no air reinforcements for overseas.

The military and political aspects of the crisis in the Middle East distracted the British cabinet up to the final week of September 1938. For too long the defensive planning for the Mediterranean had been neglected. What should the fleet do in this crisis? Keep open the Red Sea for reinforcements from India? Concentrate in the eastern Mediterranean to interrupt Italian communications with Libya? Defend Malta? How could Italian vulnerability be exploited?

These questions were still undecided by the time of the Munich crisis because the answer depended upon French co-operation. Staff talks that had taken place during the summer of 1938 excluded discussion of the Mediterranean and Italian hostility at British insistence. Neither the British nor the French had any idea of the others' intentions. The best information came when General Gamelin visited London. Only then did the British learn that France expected that a hostile Italy would tie down forces which should be used against Germany. Fifteen

French divisions would have to be kept in Tunisia and the French Alps. In addition, no consideration had been given to the effect of a neutral Italy on plans for economic warfare against Germany. Italy would probably act as a channel for German trade.

A major incentive towards resolving the Czechoslovak crisis on Hitler's terms was not only British weakness in air defense, the exaggerated estimates of German air power, and the fear of a "knock-out" blow, but also a fear of a concurrent crisis in the eastern Mediterranean and of a Japanese move against western interests in the Far East. The uppermost fact in the minds of British strategists was the possibility of a simultaneous war in three areas of the empire. Britain's limited forces were divided among theaters which strained them to the limit. British military planners were convinced that they were facing war with Hitler on unfavorable terms plus a number of possible disasters in the overseas empire. This was how the situation appeared in London, regardless of whether it was true. To the Chamberlain government, the threat to the British empire loomed as large as the threat on the other side of the English Channel.

Britain did gain some benefits from the September crisis, however. The British military services were able to test their defenses and their mobilization plans; and, in the year's delay gained by the Munich Agreement, British military power increased—as did Germany's. But the French failed to make efficient use of the time. There was a slight increase in aircraft production, which the government exaggerated; but the nation continued to suffer from internal problems, with generally poor productivity throughout the armament industries and with the trade unions directly opposing the acceleration of armaments production.

The Soviet Union (particularly Joseph Stalin) benefitted greatly from the Munich Conference, for the Soviet government was able to pose as a firm opponent of nazism and, at the same time, evade its obligations to Czechoslovakia. Nevertheless, western powers have been severely criticized by some for their failure to turn to Stalin for help. These critics have interpreted Maxim Litvinov's pious declarations in behalf of collective security to mean that Soviet aid against Hitler would be readily available if requested. However, as Stalin's spokesman, Litvinov was careful not to commit his master to any action that might require the use of military force, for Stalin had never been as eager to aid Czechoslovakia against Nazi Germany as some had imagined. The pacts that Litvinov had negotiated with Czechoslovakia and France were intended only to protect Russia from possible German attacks; they were not intended as a definite Russian commitment to either France or Czechoslovakia. In diplomatic conferences, Soviet representatives avoided explaining precisely how their country might aid Czechoslovakia, and they always tacked qualifying conditions onto what promises they did make. When questioned about Soviet assistance to Czechoslovakia, Litvinov was careful to make Soviet assistance dependent upon prior approval by the Council of the League of Nations, a process guaranteed to produce procrastination and inaction.

At the time of the crisis in September 1938, Russia made no military preparations in case Czechoslovakia required help, because Stalin had no intention of sending aid. Because of the massive purge of the Soviet armed forces, the deployment of Soviet troops outside the Soviet borders would be out of the question. Litvinov disappeared from public view late in September, reappearing on October 1—after the crisis was over—to denounce Britain and France. If they had stood firm he claimed, "they would, with Russian help, have made Hitler climb down."[16] But he had offered no help when it could have been used. In June, Litvinov had criticized the western powers and indicated that the Soviet Union could not be responsible for future developments, and in August, he had notified Berlin that the Soviet Union considered the Sudeten question an internal affair of Czechoslovakia and not a matter that would concern Moscow. Litvinov always fell back on the excuse that there was no way for Soviet aid to reach Czechoslovakia because the Soviet Union and Czechoslovakia lacked a common border. By September 24, however, the Kremlin received notification that the Rumanian government had agreed to permit the passage of Soviet troops through its country and to allow Soviet planes to traverse Rumanian airspace en route to Czechoslovakia. The Soviet government neither replied to the Rumanian offer nor informed the Czechoslovak and French governments of the Rumanian action.

In looking back on the situation, it was certainly true that neither Britain nor France was prepared for war. In Britain, only the Royal Navy had any degree of combat readiness, and the R.A.F. was faced with a shortage of new planes, weapons, and pilots. Anti-aircraft guns and searchlights were in short supply. And, most important of all, the radar chain that was to save Britain in 1940 had not yet been completed in 1938. Although France possessed a larger army than Germany, the French generals planned in case of war to hold their troops within the Maginot Line while Polish and German armies finished off Czechoslovakia. The French General Staff had made no plans for joint action with either Czechoslovakia or Britain.

But it is also true that the German military, although ready for a blitzkrieg war against Czechoslovakia, was unprepared for a full-scale world war in 1938. Along the Czechoslovak borders, there were thirty-seven divisions, but only five divisions were available to protect Germany from an invasion by France. There were inadequate forces to withstand any attack through East Prussia. The Luftwaffe was strong enough to attack Czechoslovakia but it could put up only a weak defense in the west.

Finally, the fact that there was peace instead of war as a result of the Munich Agreement pleased those people in Europe who believed that the Sudeten cause was just and that a war in behalf of Czechoslovakia was immoral. They were convinced that peace was worth the price of ceding the Sudetenland to Germany. In their longing to avoid war, it appeared moral to them to sacrifice the security of the Czechoslovak people to appease Hitler and give Europe peace.

Hitler, however, was unhappy over the outcome of the Munich Conference because he had been denied his short war; he had to settle for the Sudetenland, the cause of which he had championed publicly, instead of his true goal: a war to destroy Czechoslovakia. Trapped by his own propaganda, he had to change his plans. Never again would he permit anyone to cheat him out of a war by concocting a compromise as Chamberlain had done. He came to regard the Munich Agreement as a mistake.

In 1945, sitting in the Reichschancellery bunker, pondering the reasons for the defeat of the Third Reich, he voiced his regret over the failure of his policy at Munich. "We ought to have gone to war in 1938. . . . At Munich we lost a unique opportunity of easily and swiftly winning a war that was in any case inevitable. . . . September 1938 would have been the most favorable date."[17]

THE END OF CZECHOSLOVAKIA

Although the appeasers celebrated the Munich Agreement, the cession of the Sudetenland was only a temporary measure as far as Hitler was concerned. He was simply waiting for his next opportunity to destroy Czechoslovakia. Consequently, at every opportunity German troops acting under Hitler's orders pushed past the limits of the occupation zone specified by the Munich Agreement. Once they had occupied Czechoslovak territory, it became German.

Except for a few vain efforts from the Czech delegate, the five-power international commission—consisting of Germany, Italy, France, Britain, and Czechoslovakia—that had been established to supervise the implementation of the Munich Agreement offered no protest. German diplomats and generals dominated the meetings. In determining the final frontier, the international commission, at Ribbentrop's insistence, used a 1910 census that was more favorable to Germany than a later one would have been. And the settlement was complicated by the incursions of German troops past the limits of the occupation zone. Once they had violated the temporary frontier, Hitler forbade their withdrawal. Because it was unthinkable that German troops would give up territory they had occupied, the frontier was finally decided not by the international commission but by a German ultimatum giving Czechoslovakia a forty-eight-hour time limit to accept the frontier as determined by the German troops. After the Czechs capitulated, the international commission solemnly ratified the frontier.

But the Czech-Sudeten minority problem had not been settled. Rather, it had been further complicated, because there were still many Sudetens remaining within Czechoslovakia. Hitler had not wanted plebiscites to determine the future of these Sudetens: by leaving them in Czechoslovakia, he would have an additional minority problem to exploit if he needed it. In addition to this, however, there were thousands of Czechs caught within the new German frontiers. By mutual consent of Germany and Czechoslovakia, the Munich Agreement provisions for plebiscites were ignored, since the results of plebiscites could have altered the frontiers drastically to the detriment of either or both countries, thus disrupting the plans of Hitler's generals and creating new minority problems for the Czechoslovak government.

As it was, the concessions to Germany brought demands for concessions from Czechoslovakia's neighbors. Poland and Hungary, at Hitler's urging, used their national minorities within Czechoslovakia to obtain territory for themselves. Poland's pretension to the status of a great power had been ignored by the planners of the Munich Conference. But the cession of the Sudetenland had opened the way for Beck to obtain the status he sought by dispatching an ultimatum to Prague on September 30 demanding the cession of Teschen, the area taken from Poland in 1920. Under pressure from London and Paris, the Czechs again complied. Because Poland could not have acquired Teschen without Hitler, Poland became indebted to him. And Hitler would expect repayment of the debt.

The breakup of Czechoslovakia continued with Hungarian claims for the territory that was occupied by Magyars. No loss of territory had angered the Hungarians more than the land that had been taken from them in 1919 to extend the southern frontier of Slovakia. Because the Hungarians had not pushed their claims hard enough to satisfy him, Hitler did not press their cause at the Munich Conference, forcing Hungary to resort to its own negotiations with Czechoslovakia. After these negotiations collapsed in October, both countries appealed to the Munich powers to settle the dispute. Britain and France chose to relinquish all responsibility in the matter to Germany and Italy, thereby magnifying the prestige of the Fascist powers. Ribbentrop and Ciano, acting for their governments on November 2, decided in favor of Hungary, giving the Magyar state a territory with a population of over one million people.

Eager to take advantage of the friendly atmosphere of the Munich Conference, Chamberlain began to work out an economic approach to appeasement. He hoped that he could pacify Germany by granting economic advantages, thereby making Germany's territorial grabs unnecessary. Britain offered Germany large credits and proposed new agreements on Anglo-German trade that would be extremely beneficial to Germany. In negotiations, the Germans were astounded at the eagerness of British trade delegations to reach an agreement. However, negotiations achieved very little. Chamberlain had adopted his conciliatory attitude, imagining that once economic relations favored Germany, confidence in Europe would be restored and peace would be strengthened through new opportunities for trade and commerce. But Hitler, who did not think exclusively in economic terms, regarded the British offers as further signs that there would be no opposition to further aggression.

When Bonnet sought a Franco-German declaration similar to the one Chamberlain had signed with Hitler on September 30, Chamberlain could not raise any objection. The suggestion was welcome in Berlin, for Hitler wanted a French promise to keep hands off his intrigues in eastern Europe. Consequently Hitler sent his personal plane to bring the French ambassador, Andre François-Poncet, to Berchtesgaden for a conference. To prove that he was a Francophile, Hitler denounced the British for causing the recent trouble over Czechoslovakia, and he appeared eager to reconcile himself with France. After this friendly meeting, the subject was pursued by the foreign ministries. By early November, the German Foreign Ministry had prepared a draft declaration for Bonnet's consideration. Despite the French Foreign Minister's desire to have an early signing of the declarations, negotiations continued into December.

The Franco-German declaration which had been drafted in Berlin was finally signed on December 6. Ribbentrop represented Germany, and Bonnet represented France. The terms seemed innocent. Both countries acknowledged that no territorial question was outstanding, and both recognized their frontiers as final. Should there be troublesome international matters, both promised to confer. However, the talks that accompanied the signing revealed the meaning of the declaration. Ribbentrop asserted that Czechoslovakia lay within Germany's sphere of influence, and any French agreement to guarantee the integrity of the new Czechoslovakia would be looked upon as an attempt to wreck the Franco-German declaration. Friendship between France and Germany, according to Ribbentrop, was entirely dependent upon French acknowledgment of German hegemony in eastern Europe. During the conference, Bonnet had never challenged Ribbentrop's declaration; and, by his silence, he had implied consent to it.

The Franco-German declaration, like Chamberlain's drive for economic appeasement of Germany, only encouraged Hitler in his campaign to smash Czechoslovakia, a campaign that had been halted momentarily by the Munich Conference. Shortly after the signing of the Munich Agreement, Hitler had inquired about the forces Germany would need to destroy Czechoslovak resistance. How much time would be required to move in additional troops? How much warning would the troops need to go into action? On October 21, 1938, after he had collected the answers to these questions, Hitler issued a directive for the Wehrmacht to prepare for the "liquidation" of Czechoslovakia whenever a favorable opportunity should develop. To avoid having to mobilize additional troops, thereby arousing foreign opinion, he ordered a high degree of combat readiness for the standing army. He issued a supplement to the directive in December, explaining that the liquidation must appear to be a pacification measure and not a military operation.

Throughout the winter of 1938–1939, Hitler continued his pressure on Czechoslovakia, complaining that the Czechoslovak army was too large and should be reduced, that the Prague government did not persecute the Jews as they should, and that too much of the Benes mentality remained in the nation.

For the Czechoslovak people in their winter of misery, one hope remained—the guarantee by the Munich powers of the Czechoslovak frontiers against unprovoked aggression. Despite the attempts of Britain and France, however, this guarantee was destined never to be implemented. In order to make it palatable to Hitler, Chamberlain pressured Daladier and Bonnet to accept his interpretation of the guarantee, which was that it must have the backing of at least three of the four powers, so that Britain and France would not have to go to war against Germany and Italy over Czechoslovakia. With France in their pockets, Chamberlain and Halifax took a trip to Rome in January 1939 to try to convert Mussolini to their viewpoint, but the Duce found excuses to avoid joining in the guarantee. When the British and French governments brought up the subject in Berlin, the Fuehrer claimed that an implementation of the guarantee would serve only to foment Czechoslovak hostility towards Germany.

Hitler insisted on waiting until some of the internal problems of Czechoslovakia had been settled and relations with its neighbors had improved. Hitler's categorical reply on March 3, 1939, was reason enough for Chamberlain and Daladier to cease their efforts at implementation.

Hitler avoided this guarantee because he did not want to tie himself down with yet another agreement. He was waiting for his chance to devour the remainder of Czechoslovakia, and he knew the greater the insurance of peace there, the less chance he would have to act.

Hitler found the key to the final destruction of Czechoslovakia in the Slovak minority. The Slovaks had been granted autonomy on October 6, 1938, and their premier was Monsignor Joseph Tiso, who practiced a Slovak brand of fascism. Berlin encouraged Tiso to push for complete separation. Hitler even hinted that, if the Slovaks asked him to protect their independence, he would gladly comply. With this encouragement, the Slovaks demanded that Prague permit them their own army and give them greater financial aid. The Prague government finally began to realize that, unless the Tiso government was curbed, Czechoslovakia would degenerate into a confederation and might eventually be dissolved entirely. Prague decided to be firm, thereby providing Hitler with the opportunity he had been seeking.

On March 10, 1939, Prague dismissed the Tiso government, proclaimed martial law in Slovakia, and appointed Karol Sidor to succeed Tiso. Unable to persuade Sidor to proclaim independence, the Nazis called on Hitler for help. Berlin decided that it was necessary to continue to recognize Tiso as the legal premier. Ordering Tiso to Berlin, Hitler launched into one of his harangues. If the Slovaks wanted independence, he was willing to help and protect them, but should the Slovaks reject him, Hitler would leave them to the mercy of Hungary. Provided with a "declaration of independence" drafted by Ribbentrop and grateful for Hitler's benevolence, Tiso returned to Slovakia. He delivered the declaration of independence to the Slovak cabinet and diet and informed them of Hitler's wishes. Sidor was obliged to resign. After the cabinet and the diet unanimously approved the "independence" requested by Berlin, Hitler had his excuse to march into Czechoslovakia; he was protecting the right of self-determination.

To speed the fall of Czechoslovakia, Ribbentrop sent the Hungarian minister home to Budapest to inform his government that the time had come for them to occupy Ruthenia, the extreme eastern section of Czechoslovakia. The Hungarian government was excited at the prospect, but preferred that Germany move first. When they received news of the Slovak proclamation, Budapest dispatched an ultimatum to Prague requiring the evacuation of Ruthenia within twenty-four hours. Budapest also demanded the arming of Magyar inhabitants. Prague accepted the ultimatum but would not arm the Magyars, so Budapest found the reply unsuitable. At dawn on March 15, Hungarian troops crossed into Ruthenia. All that was left of Czechoslovakia now was a part of Bohemia and Moravia, home of the Czechs.

By March 11, an ultimatum to Prague had been drafted in Berlin, but the Czech government was not, as yet, aware of Hitler's precise intentions. On instructions from Berlin, the German minister in Prague had been unavailable to Czech officials; and since March 13, the Czech minister in Berlin had been denied information about German intentions. In desperation, Emil Hacha, the president of Czechoslovakia, requested an audience with Hitler. Already German troops had seized towns across the Czech frontier, but Hitler received the aged president early in the morning of March 15.

Hitler put on the performance that had been denied him at Munich. He berated Hacha for the Czech hostility toward Germany and grieved over the iniquities of the ungrateful Czechs who persisted in the policies of Benes. Finally he told Hacha that German troops had been ordered to begin occupying Bohemia and Moravia at 6:00 A.M. Hitler offered Hacha a choice: the Czechs could resist and be annihilated or they could accept their fate without resistance and be permitted a limited degree of national freedom. As usual with these meetings, all the necessary documents had been carefully prepared in advance. Hitler demanded that Hacha and Frantisek Chvalkovsky, the Czech Foreign Minister, sign the document and then left Goering and Ribbentrop to finish the job. Goering and Ribbentrop subjected the Czechs to shouts, curses, and insults. Twice Hacha fainted; and, at last exhausted by the ordeal, he surrendered and agreed to sign the documents. After telephone connections were established with Prague, he directed the Czech premier, Rudolf

Beran, not to resist the occupying forces. Hacha and Chvalkovsky had been browbeaten into turning the Czech people over to Hitler and surrendering all of the Czech armed forces. The documents they had signed were merely for appearance, a formality undergone to show the world that Germany had not attacked Czechoslovakia. According to the published communique, Hacha and Chvalkovsky had taken the step only after a frank consultation with Hitler. By this charade, Hitler presented France and Britain with a fait accompli, preventing a repetition of the Munich Conference in which Chamberlain might have become too zealous about Czechoslovak interests.

At dawn on March 15, the weather was so poor that the planes of the Luftwaffe were unable to take off; but, by 9:00 A.M., German soldiers had entered Prague. The same day, German troops occupied the newly "independent" Slovakia; and by evening, Hitler was in the president's palace in Prague, where he issued a proclamation formally ending Czechoslovak independence.

In the face of Hitler's fait accompli, Britain and France could only protest for the record book. Neither country was willing to go to war even though Hitler's action had, in effect, torn up the Munich Agreement. Both countries, by appeasing Hitler and presenting the territory to him as a sphere of influence, had led Hitler to believe that they had written off Czechoslovakia entirely. But this had not been their intent. The appeasers had hoped that Hitler would be reasonable and seek conciliation to avoid a war as disastrous as the last. To do their share of being conciliatory, the appeasers had stretched the concept of self-determination as far as it would stretch, and they had laboriously constructed a defense for Hitler's aggression. Now, by his takeover of Czechoslovakia, he had destroyed their edifice. In the words of Bonnet, "The peace and appeasement policy of the 'men of Munich' had suffered a lamentable disaster. And now in every country warmongers who would lead Europe toward catastrophe were bound to gain the upper hand."[18]

Hitler had promised Chamberlain that he only wanted the return of Germans to the Fatherland, but the occupation of Czechoslovakia shattered that pretense. With that promise broken and with the policy of appeasement shattered, Chamberlain was faced with a political crisis. He still wanted to practice appeasement if Hitler would only let him; if Hitler would not permit appeasement, then he must begin to build some other policy, preferably continuing to avoid war.

After Halifax and others in the cabinet and in Parliament prevailed upon him to speak out against Hitler's action, Chamberlain voiced his first public warning on March 17. Was Hitler's action in Czechoslovakia "a step in the direction of an attempt to dominate the world by force?" If Hitler intended such a challenge, he must not imagine that "because it believes war to be a senseless and evil thing, this nation has so lost its fibre that it will not take part to the utmost of its power resisting such a challenge if it were ever made."[19] No longer would Hitler be trusted. A new policy was required.

NOTES

1 Friedrich Rainer testimony, *Trials of the Major War Criminals* (Nuremberg, 1946), XVI, p. 124.

2 Kurt von Schuschnigg, *Austrian Requiem* (New York, 1946), p. 24.

3 Hitler to Mussolini, March 11, 1938, *Documents on German Foreign Policy*, Series D, I, p. 575.

4 *Nazi Conspiracy and Agression* (Washington, 1946), V, p. 642.

5 Halifax to Palairet, March 11, 1938, *Documents on British Foreign Policy*, Third Series, I, p. 13.

6 Bullitt to Hull, May 22, 1938, *Foreign Relations of the United States, 1938*, I, pp. 512–515.

7 Phipps to Halifax, May 22, 1938, *Documents on British Foreign Policy*, Third Series, I, p. 340.

8 Wiedemann memorandum, *Documents on German Foreign Policy*, Series D, VII, p. 632.

9 *Directive for Operation Green*, May 30, 1938, in ibid., II, p. 358.

10 Bonnet's note on his conversation with Osusky, *Documents Diplomatiques Francais*, 2d series (1936–1939), vol. X, p. 437–438.

11 *Documents on International Affairs*, 1938 (London, 1943), II, p. 193.

12 Neville Chamberlain, *In Search of Peace* (New York, 1939), pp. 174–175.

13 Parliamentary Debates, House of Commons, Fifth Series, vol. 339, cols. 26–28.

14 The Anglo-German Declaration, September 30, 1938, *Documents on German Foreign Policy*, Series D, II, p. 107.

15 Chamberlain, op. cit., p. 174.

16 Phipps to Halifax, October 1, 1938, *Documents on British Foreign Policy*, Third Series, III, p. 67.

17 Hugh Trevor-Roper, editor, *The Testament of Adolf Hitler: The Hitler-Bormann Documents* (London: Cassel, 1961), p. 84.

18 Welczek to the German Foreign Ministry, *Documents on German Foreign Policy*, Series D, IV, p. 283.

19 Chamberlain, op. cit., pp. 274–275.

5 / WAR, 1939

DANZIG

The German occupation of Czechoslovakia meant that Poland was surrounded by Germany on three frontiers; and, with vital areas open to attack, Polish security was endangered. Any help from the West would have to come by sea; but, in a war involving Germany, the Baltic would literally become a German lake. In these circumstances, safety for Poland would seem to lie in seeking external protection against Germany. However, the person who was to guide Polish foreign policy through this period chose to follow other policies.

Jozef Beck, the Polish Foreign Minister, had for too long been cool to the German threat although he was not inexperienced in foreign affairs. He had been Pilsudski's *chef de cabinet*, then undersecretary in the Foreign Ministry, before finally becoming Foreign Minister in 1932. Those who had to deal with him found him sinister, inclined to be devious, and given to backstairs intrigue. He cared little for the League of Nations because it concerned itself with matters that Beck considered strictly internal concerns. The League's preoccupation with minorities, of which Poland had its share, was particularly vexing to Beck; he considered the League's supervision of Danzig as a free city an insult to Poland. He had never cared for the alliance with France—perhaps because, earlier in his career, he had been expelled from France for trying to sell French military secrets.

Beck longed for Poland to play the role of a big power, so he exaggerated Polish strength to the outside world. However, geography had played a trick on Poland; situated between Soviet Russia and Nazi Germany, a policy of independence—even of independence from France—would be difficult, if not impossible. The prospect of Germany and Soviet Russia coming to terms seemed impossible to Beck because of the great ideological gap between the two nations. But neither could he believe that Hitler would move against a nation courageous enough to fight. "Hitler," Beck told American ambassador William Bullitt in 1939, "was a timid Austrian who would not risk war against determined and strong opponents."[1]

In January 1938, when Beck became aware of Hitler's intention to destroy Austrian independence, he intimated to Hitler that Poland would not oppose *Anschluss*, hoping that Hitler would purchase Polish neutrality by solving the Danzig question. Hitler, however, ordered his troops into Austria without meeting Beck's price. Even though the deal over Austria fell through, Beck did not shrink from conniving with Hitler in the September crisis, because he considered Czechoslovakia to be an "artificial creation"[2] that was doomed to disappear. Both men agreed at that time that Czechoslovakia might become a "hotbed of bolshevism."[3] It was then also that Hitler hinted to Beck that Czechoslovakia would soon follow Austria into the Nazi empire. This news was not unpleasing to Beck who dreamed of founding a "Third Europe": a bloc of states, led by Poland and Hungary, stretching from the Baltic to the Adriatic. Because an independent Czechoslovakia blocked Beck from this goal, he joined Hitler in dissolving Czechoslovakia, with the hope that Slovakia and Ruthenia would not come under German domination.

Beck's policies during the Czechoslovak crisis seemed to reassure Hitler that, in return for Teschen, Poland would accept a position as a German satellite. If that sop proved insufficient to tame Poland, Hitler had no doubt that the Poles would understand the lesson to be learned from Czechoslovakia's fate—that Britain and France could not be relied upon to fight to uphold the Versailles treaty. Like Czechoslovakia, after putting up a bold front, Poland would concede.

While the Munich victory was still fresh, Hitler's campaign against Poland got underway. On October 24, Jozef Lipski, the Polish ambassador, met with Ribbentrop at a restaurant in Berchtesgaden at the Foreign Minister's request. Following Beck's instructions, Lipski began by arguing the case for Hungary annexing Ruthenia, which was inhabited largely by Ukrainians, Magyars, and a few Rumanians. The annexation of Ruthenia was central to Beck's dream of a "Third Europe," because it would help to make Poland and Hungary independent of Germany and Soviet Russia. But Hitler refused to surrender such a useful pawn unless his policy would benefit. Moreover, Beck's "Third Europe" plan would help in the creation of an anti-German bloc of states. Ribbentrop, however, said that he would need more time to consider the annexation at his leisure. Then he turned to the reason for this meeting.

The problem which he was about to broach should be kept in the strictest confidence between Lipski, Beck, and himself. According to Ribbentrop, who was following the instructions of his master, the time had come to arrive at a general settlement of potential sources of friction between Germany and Poland. Consequently it was necessary to speak about Danzig. "Danzig was German—had always been German, and would always remain German," Ribbentrop informed Lipski.[4] He proposed that Danzig come under German rule, and that a railroad and a highway with extraterritorial rights be constructed across the Polish Corridor to Danzig. Further, Germany and Poland would guarantee their frontiers, and Poland would join the Anti-Comintern Pact, placing itself in opposition to Soviet Russia. Lipski, surprised, could only declare that Danzig was almost a symbol. Beck, he declared, could never make the Polish people accept Danzig being ceded to Germany. Ribbentrop, trying to be diplomatic, assured Lipski that he did not need an immediate answer.

If, however, Beck accepted these terms, they would symbolize Polish commitment to Hitler's cause and the end of the Polish alliance with France. In effect, Poland would cease being a free agent and become a German satellite. The end result of this proposal would be to turn Poland into a German vassal who would remain quiet while Hitler settled scores with Britain and France before embarking on a campaign to seize *Lebensraum* in eastern Europe. Beck's "Third Europe" dream had been shattered.

On November 19, Lipski reported to Ribbentrop that Beck had rejected the October 24 proposal concerning German right to Danzig, and he submitted a counterproposal, offering to expand the 1934 nonaggression pact and to replace the League of Nations' guarantee of Danzig's international status with a

Polish-German guarantee. Beck implied that any attempt at incorporating Danzig into Germany would lead to war. Ribbentrop accepted the Polish rejection good-naturedly, assuring Lipski that Germany wanted as good relations with Poland as possible; all of his efforts were directed towards that goal. Ribbentrop was surprised, he claimed, that Beck considered Hitler's proposals harmful to Polish-German relations and asked that Beck reconsider them, for they were intended only to remove points of friction between the two countries.

But, throughout the following months, Beck would not budge, because he knew that these concessions would spell the end of Polish independence. Beck, however, had not learned from the example of Czechoslovakia. He imagined that obstinacy could be a substitute for guns and tanks. He did not believe that Hitler would dare to go to war. To the contrary, Hitler began moving toward forceful takeover when, on November 24, he issued a revised directive ordering preparations for a surprise occupation of Danzig whenever a suitable occasion appeared. Faced with a fait accompli, the Poles would speak less bravely.

Meanwhile, "negotiations" would continue. Beck wangled a personal meeting with Hitler on January 5, 1939; and the Fuehrer, not yet ready to give Beck the treatment he had given Schuschnigg and Hacha, was on his best behavior. Hitler conceded that a strong Poland was necessary for Germany because of the Russian danger, but he insisted that Danzig was a German city and must be returned to the Reich. Hitler indicated that he was prepared to guarantee Poland's frontiers, including the Polish Corridor, but Beck was willing only to promise a continuation of the existing policy of avoiding dependence on Soviet Russia. As for Danzig, Beck stalled for more time; it was a difficult question, and he had to think of Polish public opinion.

On the second day of the meeting, Ribbentrop repeated the October demands, but Beck would concede nothing. He asked Ribbentrop to inform Hitler that there were no grounds for an agreement. Ribbentrop, however, assured Beck that Germany would not resort to force because it wanted friendly relations with Poland. Beck then left Berlin without an agreement and without concessions, but he left negotiations open. The last attempt at persuasion made by Ribbentrop came when he visited Beck in Warsaw on January 25 through 27. Although Beck refused all of Ribbentrop's proposals over Danzig, there was still no break in relations. Ribbentrop did not force the issue, and Beck did not reject further discussion. Hitler, however, knew that friendly persuasion would have to give way to more forceful methods if Poland were to be brought into the German orbit.

Although Beck did not reveal the content of these talks to London and Paris, nevertheless, the rumor soon appeared that he had made a deal with Hitler. And Beck did not attempt to correct the misapprehensions: he kept silent lest Britain and France pressure him into concessions as they had done with Benes. By remaining silent yet rejecting Hitler's demands, Beck hoped to be able to settle the German-Polish problem without war and at the same time avoid a Munich-type conference over Poland.

When, on March 15, German troops occupied Bohemia and Moravia, Beck at first did not seem alarmed that German troops were dangerously near Polish borders, and he complained only about German machine guns being trained on Polish territory. He claimed to be happy over the "independence" of Slovakia and hoped that events of March 15 would aid Polish-German relations. But his elation could not obscure the ominous presence of German troops, which now flanked Poland on three sides. He did not hesitate to protest the establishment of a German protectorate over Slovakia—a major blow to his scheme for a Third Europe.

A new threat to European stability appeared when Viorel Tilea, the Rumanian minister, informed Halifax on March 17 of the imminent German aggression against Rumania. He explained that, in the course of economic negotiations, the German delegation had handed his government an ultimatum demanding a monopoly of Rumanian exports and a restriction on Rumanian production that would be favorable to German interests, in return for which Germany promised to "guarantee" the Rumanian frontiers. Tilea begged for British aid if Rumania should become a victim of German aggression. At any moment, he explained, German troops might attack. He thought the situation might be saved "if it was possible to construct a solid block of Poland, Rumania, Greece, Turkey, Yugoslavia with the support of Great Britain and France."[5]

Although Tilea's story was exaggerated, it contained enough truth to alarm Chamberlain and Halifax. Germany intended the German-Rumanian economic agreement to be the foundation of a German sphere of influence in southeastern Europe involving not only Rumania, but also Yugoslavia, Bulgaria, Hungary, and Turkey. But there were also political goals, according to Helmut Wohltat, who negotiated for Germany: "The political development of the national states in southeastern Europe will follow the German pattern to an increasing extent, while the influence of western European democracies and the Soviet Union would be eliminated."[6]

The British Foreign Office responded on March 17 by asking Warsaw, Ankara, Athens, Belgrade, Paris, and Moscow what their attitude would be should Rumania suffer German aggression. Only Paris would promise to help. In Moscow, Litvinov disdained to share his opinion, but asked for a conference in Bucharest to discuss the possibilities of common action before the event. Halifax refused to send a cabinet minister halfway across Europe for a time-consuming conference when there seemed to be no assurance of success.

Suddenly faced with Tilea's story, Chamberlain was spurred on to a new foreign policy, which he considered to be necessary before negotiations could be resumed with Hitler. What Chamberlain called a "pretty bold and startling plan"[7] involved a declaration by Poland, France, Britain, and the Soviet Union that, whenever the political independence of any European nation was threatened, the four governments would consult on joint action to resist the threat. Chamberlain intended this declaration to force Hitler to desist from further aggression and return to the conference table. It would also encourage the small states, when threatened with aggression, to refuse to make the concessions that Hitler demanded. While this "new" policy was still not strong enough to deter Hitler, Chamberlain considered it radical because Britain was making a promise in advance.

This proposed declaration was not to Beck's liking. Still hopeful of keeping Hitler contented, the Polish Foreign Minister scorned any public declaration made in association with the Soviet government because Berlin might interpret such a statement as proof that Poland had joined the Soviet camp. Instead, fearing that once the British and French were aware of Hitler's demands they would pressure him to concede as they had done with Czechoslovakia, Beck insisted on a secret bilateral treaty with Britain, while concealing the German demands from London. The bilateral agreement was not to Halifax's liking; he and Chamberlain proffered an arrangement in which Britain and France would come to the aid of Poland and Rumania—provided Poland and Rumania would aid each other and keep London and Paris informed on all developments that threatened their independence. Before this proposal could be acted on, Hitler moved again.

By the spring of 1939, Hitler had gained no further ground in his quest to turn Poland into a vassal. He tried again by capitalizing on the occupation of Bohemia and Moravia. On March 21, Lipski was summoned to another meeting with Ribbentrop; the friendly attitude of the earlier conference was missing. The Foreign Minister presented the German explanation of the occupation of Bohemia and Moravia. Lipski informed Ribbentrop that in Poland the announcement that Germany had become the protector of Slovakia troubled the average person.

Then Ribbentrop suggested that Beck pay an early visit to Berlin. After all, the Fuehrer was the only one who could renounce the German claim to the Polish Corridor. But the condition for renouncing this claim would be the return of Danzig to Germany and the building of an extraterritorial railroad and highway across the Corridor to East Prussia. In return, Germany would guarantee the Corridor. The Fuehrer had been amazed at Poland's strange attitude, Ribbentrop warned. He must not form an impression that Poland was simply unwilling to reach a settlement.

While Lipski was in Warsaw conferring with Beck, Hitler was not idle. On March 23, Germany and Rumania signed the trade treaty, Slovakia officially became a German protectorate, and German troops occupied Memel, the chief port of Lithuania, which had been a German city before the Versailles treaty. This capitulation came about as a result of threats from Ribbentrop that Lithuania would fare better from a peaceful solution to its territorial dispute than from a military one; Lithuania agreed to evacuate the territory. Clearly, the move was intended to frighten the Poles, for Britain and France had no vital interest in Memel, and Germany could easily have recaptured the territory at any time. It succeeded in its intent: the Warsaw government was alarmed, immediately called up reservists, while Polish newspapers attacked Beck for his shortsightedness in dealing with Hitler, and critics in parliament joined in the assault. Faced with such opposition, Beck dared not seek accommodation with Hitler.

On March 25, Hitler had not yet fully made up his mind about Poland, according to a memorandum of a talk the Fuehrer had with General Brauchitsch. Hitler wanted a military solution of the Danzig question only if Poland would not cede it voluntarily; and he still clung to the hope that Beck would fall into line, for he wished to avoid pushing Poland into the arms of Britain. If he had to resort to a military solution, then a "coup" would have to be planned that would present the world with a fait accompli. Hitler ordered work on the final solution of the Polish problem to begin, with the instruction that "Poland would have to be so beaten down that during the next few decades, she need not be taken into account as a political factor."[8]

But the Memel coup had frightened the Warsaw government into believing that Danzig would be next. Under these circumstances, a hard-line policy was necessary to keep Hitler in check. He must understand that Poland would fight over Danzig.

When Lipski returned to Berlin on March 26 with Beck's answer to the demands made on March 21, he received a cold reception from Ribbentrop. Beck, so he reported, was willing to study improvement in transportation between Germany and East Prussia, but Germany could have no extraterritorial rights in the Polish Corridor. Beck was agreeable to a Polish-German guarantee of Danzig. Unhappy because there had been no move toward concession, Ribbentrop retorted that a settlement was possible only on a basis of the German demands, and that there could be no counterproposals. On March 28, caught between Hitler's inflexible demands and the mounting pressure from the Polish patriots, Beck warned Berlin that any German change in the administration of Danzig would be considered reason enough for Poland to go to war.

In London, the rumors of imminent war between Germany and Poland prodded Halifax and Chamberlain into action. Twice Halifax announced to the Polish ambassador that if the Danzig question became a threat to Polish independence, "His Majesty's Government would have to treat it as a question which was of the gravest concern to themselves."[9] By March 27, Halifax and Chamberlain extracted a pledge from the cabinet to promise aid to Poland and Rumania if either were in danger of German aggression, provided each assisted the other. Even the Secret Intelligence Service had received reports (all erroneous) that German preparations for an attack on Poland were to be concluded on March 28. Then Ian Colvin, a correspondent of the *London News Chronicle*, newly returned from Germany, came to the Foreign Office at the urging of the British military attaché in Berlin with an alarming story. His German contacts had indicated to him that Hitler intended to use the Danzig and Corridor problems to march on Poland at any time. Halifax had Colvin repeat his tale to Chamberlain. Imagining that they faced a sudden attack on Poland, Halifax and Chamberlain decided that now a swift, clear warning to Hitler was essential. This warning should take the form of a public pledge by Britain and France to support Poland if its independence were threatened.

Although their information did not indicate an impending coup, the Daladier government reluctantly agreed to the pledge, and it was presented to Beck. Faced with a proposal for a British and French guarantee, Beck pondered briefly and then accepted. He had not wanted this originally, but Hitler's demands, combined with the other pressures he faced—the activities of the Danzig Nazis, the Memel coup, and the pressure from within Poland to resist Hitler—led him finally to accept the pledge.

As a result of a peculiar series of decisions, the impossible had become a fact: a British government had committed itself to intervene in Central Europe. On March 31, in response to a question about the European situation, Chamberlain announced to the House of Commons that the government believed any question could be solved by peaceful means. But, in order to make the government's position perfectly clear, he declared:

> . . . in the event of any action which clearly threatened Polish independence, and which the Polish government accordingly considered it vital to resist with their national forces, His Majesty's government would feel themselves bound at once to lend the Polish government all support in their power.[10]

Chamberlain's statement, often described as a revolution in British foreign policy, was also a revolution in tactics. During the Czechoslovak crisis, Britain had given no specific pledge to aid Czechoslovakia directly, but its intervention then had depended on France first becoming involved in a war. Surely a definite warning of British intention to support Poland, given in advance, would make Hitler pause, reflect on the consequences, and then return to negotiations.

The guarantee was also intended to deter Hitler from fresh acts of aggression and, by obtaining a reciprocal guarantee from Poland, to ensure that if war came Germany would have to fight on two fronts. The British Chiefs of Staff had concluded that if Britain had to fight Germany, it was better to do so with Poland as an ally rather than after Germany had absorbed it. While admitting that nothing could be done for Poland, the Chiefs argued that a two-front war would prevent Germany from concentrating its forces along one border.

The Polish guarantee was chiefly Chamberlain's idea. He hoped that it would give Britain enough leverage to force Poland to agree to Hitler's terms over the Polish Corridor and Danzig. In Chamberlain's mind, Britain was guaranteeing Poland's independence, not its borders. The British government would judge whether Polish independence was threatened. If Polish boundaries were redrawn in Germany's favor that would not precipitate British action, but Chamberlain did not mean for this to indicate that he had drawn a line in the sand. Chamberlain hoped that Hitler would be satisfied without Poland being forced to endure a full-scale invasion or accepting a treaty that would turn its into a vassal state.

To prevent Beck from considering the pledge a blank check to make unlimited demands on Britain whenever he wished,

Halifax and Chamberlain did take steps. They requested that Beck keep London and Paris informed, and that he refrain from any action that might antagonize Hitler.

However, Chamberlain and Halifax were still living in a world that had not existed since 1914. In 1939, the only kind of warning that would have been effective would have been guns and tank formations drawn up on the frontiers of Germany, with squadrons of heavy, long-range bombers loaded for attacks on German industrial centers. Hitler knew that British troops were few—and those in service were far from Germany—and that guns, tanks, and bombers had yet to be built. Words spoken in the House of Commons would have little effect on Adolf Hitler.

Chamberlain's pledge, however, served to bolster Beck's resolve not to allow Poland to become subservient to Hitler. But during the final days of March and early April, Hitler realized that Poland would not concede to his demands that it become a German satellite. Unless Poland surrendered, Germany must attack before turning on the West. There was no alternative to a war against Poland. Consequently, on April 3, he proceeded to order plans for the invasion of Poland, to be ready for execution by September 1, 1939. A directive dated April 11 contained the basic principles for *Operation White* and outlined the tasks for the Wehrmacht. Hitler stressed surprise attack, speed, and the swift annihilation of the Polish forces in order to present Britain and France with a fait accompli.

Beck still hoped to be able to settle with Hitler by himself and so he trifled with the British. When he conferred with Chamberlain and Halifax on April 4 and 5, he was agreeable to a reciprocal aid arrangement between Poland and Britain, but he rejected Polish aid for other nations in Central Europe.

Determined to break through Hitler's unwillingness to negotiate, Beck now sought intermediaries, including the Japanese ambassador, to carry his pleas to Hitler. But Hitler, unwilling to repeat his mistake in 1938 when he had settled for his ostensible demands, now rejected all negotiations with the Poles until August 31, only hours before German soldiers attacked Poland.

Hitler responded by publicly denouncing the nonaggression pact, claiming that the Anglo-Polish arrangements had nullified it. On the same day, April 28, he confessed to the Reichstag that he had never considered the Munich Agreement as final. Further, to frighten the appeasers, he announced the end of the Anglo-German Naval Agreement of 1935. Danzig, he declared, would never become Polish; rightfully, to remove a danger to world peace, it ought to be returned to Germany.

Again, his speech was intended for foreign consumption; he hoped that his threats would have the same effect they had in the Czechoslovak affair. If he bullied enough, Britain and France would again push Germany's weak opponent into concessions, and he would intensify his pressure on Poland until Britain and France renounced their pledges of support, thereby leaving Germany completely free to have its way. But Hitler failed to realize that Beck was not Benes, and that the political repercussions of September 1938 would make Chamberlain avoid the same mistakes he had made with Czechoslovakia.

As a further move to dishearten his opponents, Hitler joined with Mussolini in the Pact of Steel, signed on May 22. Both Italy and Germany promised full aid to the other in a war, regardless of the circumstances under which the war began. Even if Germany were the aggressor, Italy was obligated to help. Nothing hid the offensive spirit of this pact, and Hitler spared nothing to give the signing the widest publicity. Mussolini, hoping that the Pact would have an effect on his feud with France, joined under the impression that there would be no general war immediately.

The next day, Hitler informed his senior officers that Germany would attack Poland at the first suitable opportunity. He confessed that it was not Danzig that was at stake, but rather the domination of Poland; actually, war was necessary in order to expand the German territory. However, he knew that he could not hope for the easy time they had in the Czechoslovak crisis; there would have to be some fighting, but they should be able to avoid a general war. Even if this did bring about a war with the western powers, he was convinced that this was the time to destroy Poland; because, in a war with Britain and France, Poland would be a danger at Germany's back.

Much of his speech to his officers dealt with the problem of Britain, whom he considered his chief enemy—for he had perceived that Britain led France. For this reason, preparations must be made for a war with Britain. They did not have to occupy themselves with Russia, he insisted, for Russia would not be likely to object to the liquidation of Poland. He hinted that an occupation of Belgium and Holland would eventually become necessary in order to secure them as bases for an attack on Britain. All efforts must be directed towards a short war, but they must nevertheless be prepared for a long one, perhaps one of ten or fifteen years' duration.

This speech indicates that Hitler had at last made up his mind to attack Poland. Hitler was not bluffing. His audience included officers upon whose help and professional advice he had to depend for carrying out his plans. They could not be fooled; he must tell them the truth—not all, but enough to prepare them for war. He had revealed much of his thinking about the future; already he was contemplating attacking Belgium and Holland in preparation for a war on Britain. Above all, he would not allow negotiations with Poland, Britain, and France to deprive him of war despite any concessions Britain and France might extract from Poland.

His audience got the message. By June 15, he had received the army's plan of operation against Poland, setting August 20 as the target date for completing Germany's preparations for war. After that date, Hitler need only give the final order for the attack on Poland.

APPEASEMENT FAILS

While the German general staff labored over plans to wipe out Poland, German diplomats followed their instructions to denounce Anglo-French support for the Poles. Because of their March 31 declaration, the British received special attention. The Germans insinuated that Britain would be responsible for a general war, that it was Britain's backing of the Poles that was preventing Germany from settling the Danzig question peacefully. They insisted that Britain must withdraw their promise of aid to Poland.

However, it seemed publicly that the British government was determined to stop Hitler. Chamberlain announced to the House of Commons on April 13 that the government had given Greece and Rumania promises of help similar to that given Poland on March 31. Daladier joined in the pledge on the same day. Chamberlain informed the House of Commons on May 12 of an agreement with Turkey wherein both governments promised aid to each other in the event of war in the Mediterranean area. On April 26, he announced the introduction of conscription for military service, the first time in British history that it would be in effect in peacetime.

Despite these signs, Chamberlain continued to search for a peaceful solution of the Polish crisis, publicly denying at every opportunity that there was an attempt at encirclement of Germany. To show his good intentions, he handed over to Germany the Czechoslovak gold that had been held in the Bank of England. Both Halifax and Chamberlain repeatedly declared that the government would back a settlement of the Polish-German dispute as long as it was arrived at by discussion; and they strongly denied that Britain had any intention of standing in the way of German economic expansion in southeastern Europe. To reinforce this outward pressure, the British, in secret meetings with German representatives, proposed economic arrangements with Germany over southeastern Europe and agreements over armaments and colonies. Sir Horace Wilson even proposed a nonaggression pact and suggested that, if all these could be achieved, Britain would be able to evade the March 31 pledge to Poland. However, the Polish problem would not be solved. The use of an Anglo-German nonaggression pact as bait led Hitler to assume that Chamberlain was still so overanxious about war that he would surrender rather than fight for Poland. But Chamberlain's search for an arrangement with Hitler was complicated by a new force in Britain. Opposition to appeasement had become louder; and voices in the House of Commons were beginning to condemn Chamberlain's policy.

In the Czechoslovak crisis, the Soviet Union had lent assistance to Germany by keeping silent, but the isolation of Poland would require an agreement between Moscow and Berlin. Although Hitler's loud opposition to bolshevism had helped bring him to power, German army officers and diplomats favored an agreement with the Soviet Union. Despite their ideological differences, Soviet diplomats and officials had, throughout the years since 1933, hinted at their interest in friendly relations with Germany. They knew that rearmament during the Weimar period could not have been achieved with such speed had it not been for the Russian help. Furthermore, the two nations had common interests that had often been overlooked: they both shared a hatred for the Versailles settlement, and they both had old scores to settle with Poland.

On March 10, 1939, before the Eighteenth Congress of the Communist Party, Joseph Stalin made his usual report in a speech that contained significant statements regarding foreign policy. According to his analysis of foreign affairs, the chief reason that the "non-aggressive states" were making concessions to the aggressors was because they had rejected "collective security, the policy of collective resistance to the aggressor and had taken up a position of non-intervention, a position of neutrality." Such a policy revealed "an eagerness, a desire, not to hinder the aggressors in their nefarious work." The western powers allowed Germany to have Austria, "despite the undertaking to defend her independence; they let her have the Sudeten region; they abandoned Czechoslovakia to her fate."

Finally, Stalin enunciated Soviet policy towards its neighbors:

> We stand for peaceful, close and friendly relations with all neighboring countries which have common frontiers with the U.S.S.R. That is our position; and we shall adhere to this position as long as these countries maintain like relations with the Soviet Union, and as long as they make no attempt to trespass, directly or indirectly, on the integrity and inviolability of the frontiers of the Soviet state.

He concluded with a warning to the Party "to be cautious and not to allow our country to be drawn into conflicts by warmongers who are accustomed to have others pull the chestnuts out of the fire for them."[11]

Was Stalin's statement a revolution in Soviet foreign policy or was he restating an old hope, agreement with Germany over Eastern Europe? He was probably attempting to warn Britain and France not to leave the Soviet Union to face Germany alone. From Berlin there was silence. Although Ribbentrop brought the speech to Hitler's attention suggesting that he be authorized to learn more about Stalin's intentions, Hitler was uninterested.

Alexei Merekalov, the Soviet ambassador, brought a message from the Kremlin to the German Foreign Ministry on April 17. Ostensibly the reason for his visit was the matter of Soviet contracts with the Skoda works in Czechoslovakia for war materials. However, Merekalov proceeded to lead Ernst von Weizsaecker, the state secretary, into a discussion of German-Polish relations and finally came around to the subject of Russo-German affairs. At last Merekalov got to the point: ideological differences, he suggested, need not be a "stumbling block" to friendly relations. "Russia had not exploited the present friction between Germany and the western democracies against us [Germany], nor did she wish to do that."[12] There was no reason for Russia and Germany not to enjoy normal relations.

In contrast to Weizsaecker's account, according to Soviet documents released in 1990 and 1992, the meeting was not the occasion of a Soviet hint at a possible rapprochement. The signal of detente was coming from the Germans. Merekalov was merely following instructions in presenting Soviet complaints concerning Germany's failure to fulfill contracts of the former Czechoslovak Skoda factories. Merekalov made no plea for improved Russo-German relations. It is quite possible that Weizsaecker's account is the more accurate.

Meanwhile, Britain and France embarked on tortuous negotiations with the Soviet government. On April 14, the British government pressed the Soviet Union to make a public declaration promising to assist any European neighbor of the Soviet Union who resisted aggression if such assistance was desired. Britain would not be involved in this declaration. France, however, made a different proposal involving France going to war against Germany if Poland or Romania were to be attacked. France would aid the Soviet Union if it were at war as a result of aiding Poland or Romania.

Litvinov replied on April 17 with a proposal for a triple alliance in which Britain, France, and the Soviet Union would aid each other in case of aggression against any of the three powers. The western neighbors of the Soviet Union, from the Baltic to the Black Sea, would be guaranteed against aggression. There would be immediate discussion about the military assistance to be given by each of the states. Britain should inform Poland that the guarantee related only to German aggression. Following the outbreak of war, the three nations would promise not to conclude a separate peace with the aggressor.

Litvinov had shown his disdain for London's vague declaration. He preferred a military alliance and intervention before German troops reach the Soviet frontiers. However, a nation such as Poland had no wish to have Soviet troops within its borders. To Halifax such an alliance would necessitate lengthy, complicated negotiations. He proposed that the Soviet government simply make a public declaration that if Britain and France became involved in a war on behalf of eastern European countries, Soviet aid would be immediately available—if so desired.

Chamberlain wanted nothing to do with an alliance lest it alienate Germany; consequently, his government pressed for a temporary pledge to deter Hitler until he relented and returned to the conference table. The British regarded the Soviet proposal as an alliance for war, and they were reticent about forcing aid on unwilling nations, particularly Poland and Romania. A mutual assistance pact might alarm these nations, push them into the German sphere, hasten the division of Europe into armed camps, and provoke Hitler into some new rash act.

Stalin continued to have doubts about British and French willingness to fight. His agents were fishing around for assurances that they—particularly the British—would stand up to Hitler. On the morning of May 3, British ambassador William Seeds assured Litvinov that Britain would go to war to help any nation to whom promises had been made and who resisted a threat to its independence. This news should have interested Stalin, for he had feared that the British and French might go back on their promises if the country to be defended surrendered quickly or was defeated, leaving the Soviet Union to face German armies on the Soviet borders.

Later that same day, Litvinov, who had for so long been sounding the call for collective security was suddenly dismissed from his post. It is certain that he was not fired because of his past actions, for he had served Stalin well, both protecting the Soviet Union and providing a moral front for Soviet foreign policy.

Litvinov's post was filled by his chief rival, Vyacheslov Molotov, since 1917 chairman of the Council of Peoples' Commissar, a believer in world revolution, who probably had a role in Litvinov's dismissal. Both men hated each other. Molotov was obstinate, blunt, deliberately rude, without charm, ruthless, and a faithful follower of Stalin's every order. Stalin probably had more in common with Molotov than with Litvinov. The appointment of Molotov indicated that Stalin would be more personally involved in the direction of Soviet foreign policy.

To some German diplomats the appointment of Molotov was a signal to Berlin of a change in Soviet foreign policy. Hitler was unconvinced. However, the replacement did not alter the official Soviet attitude. Molotov continued the demands that Litvinov had made for an alliance. In the negotiations with the Germans, both Litvinov and Molotov were considerate and polite while maintaining a tight security. In their dealings with the British and French, both could be insulting, arrogant, and suspicious—Molotov much more so than Litvinov. He humiliated the ambassadors by seating them below him and making then use their laps for writing while he looked down from behind a desk. But Molotov's external appearance was deceiving; in fact, Stalin's "trusted" aide was assisted throughout the talks by a device which recorded every word.

The pressure on Chamberlain to seek an arrangement with the Soviet government mounted. Britain and France had pledged aid to Poland, Rumania, Turkey, and Greece, threatening Hitler with a war in the west if he attacked these nations. However, to implement their promises, Britain and France needed Soviet help. They tried to wheedle a public statement from Moscow pledging that if Britain and France became involved in a war because of their promises, Soviet aid would be available—if desired. Instead, Molotov insisted on a three-power alliance with a promise to help each other and a guarantee of the nations to the west of the Soviet Union—regardless of whether they wished to be guaranteed.

Chamberlain abhorred the idea of an alliance lest it antagonize Hitler. In addition, he distrusted the Soviet Union, fearing that an alliance would drag Britain into a war of Stalin's making. Chamberlain did not want Britain to go to war simply because Hitler declared war on the Soviet Union. He preferred that the Soviet government aid nations such as Poland and

Rumania, if these countries, facing a German invasion, requested aid. After the Soviet press reported on the government's call for a three-power alliance, speakers in the House of Commons denounced the Chamberlain government for failing to take up the Soviet offer of an alliance. An early public opinion poll showed strong support for a military alliance with the Soviet Union. As for the French, Premier Daladier did not believe that an alliance with the Soviet Union would so antagonize Hitler that he would launch a war.

Chamberlain remained suspicious of Soviet intentions and doubtful of Soviet military ability. At the same time, he feared the prospect of opposing power blocs. Consequently he sought to give the Russians what they wished but at the same time avoid the concept of an alliance by substituting a statement of intentions. Why not tie the obligation to article 16 of the Covenant of the League of Nations? By this clever ruse he would avoid the appearance of an alliance in order not to antagonize Germany and at the same time give the Russians what they desired but in a different form. According to article 16, if a member of the League of Nations resorted to war, such action would be considered an act of war against all League members who would then proceed to sever trade and financial relations and to isolate the offending state. Next the Council of the League of Nations would recommend military measures to be undertaken by League members as well as contributions from member states. The League members would also support each other in this operation. By resorting to this device Chamberlain could avoid an alliance. It would merely be a system of mutual guarantees sanctioned by the League of Nations.

Faced with a choice between a breakdown in negotiations or a military alliance, Chamberlain chose a mutual assistance agreement to avoid giving the appearance of the creation of an opposing bloc which he feared would make negotiations with Hitler difficult. On May 24, the British and French informed the Kremlin that they would negotiate a mutual assistance pact and a prominent feature would be article 16 of the Covenant of the League of Nations.

When Molotov met with Seeds and the French chargé d'affaires on May 27, he had nothing but scorn for Chamberlain's proposal to involve the League of Nations. The British and French were uninterested in achieving concrete results. They wanted the negotiations to continue indefinitely in order to avoid a concrete agreement. It meant only delays, Molotov argued. While Russia was being bombed, Bolivia could block action in Geneva. The reference to the League of Nations would prevent the agreement from ever becoming operative. The two diplomats failed to convince Molotov that the reference to the League of Nations was only a matter of principle. Seeds argued that it was necessary to base the agreement on the principles of the League of Nations in order to avoid any smell of aggression. Molotov did not want words or conversations but guaranteed action.

The arguments of the French chargé and Seeds did not affect Molotov. "My words produced not the slightest effect," Seeds complained, "they seemed not to be heard or understood."[13] On another occasion he observed, "It is my fate to deal with a man totally ignorant of foreign affairs and to whom the idea of negotiation—as distinct from imposing the will of his party leader—is utterly alien.[14]

On May 30 Molotov insisted on the need to conclude a political as well as a military agreement simultaneously. Seeds observed that there was an enormous range of problems that could have to be considered, and this could not be done immediately. Molotov brought up the question of "indirect aggression," referring to the fate of Czechoslovakia which had been delivered into the control of Germany by President Hacha without a struggle. The British government, according to Seeds, was unwilling to force aid on a nation that did not desire it.

Molotov replied with a proposal, in which article 16 had been omitted, and the three powers promised to aid each other if one were at war with a European power. They would do the same if another European power threatened Belgium, Greece, Turkey, Rumania, Poland, Latvia, Estonia, and Finland, plus any other nation which requested aid. However, the British and French governments were unwilling to impose guarantees on nations who had no wish to be guaranteed, particularly the three Baltic states. As for Poland and Rumania, these governments did not wish to be mentioned. When the British and French governments agreed to list the nations to be guaranteed, they proposed adding Switzerland, Holland, and Luxembourg. Molotov refused because the Soviet Union had no diplomatic relations with Switzerland and Holland. He simply ignored Luxembourg. London and Paris eventually agreed to drop Switzerland and Holland and to list the other states in an unpublished annex.

Molotov surprised the British and French ambassadors on July 9 with the announcement that as soon as the political agreement, in effect the alliance, had been concluded, the articles would be initialed, and then they must commence negotiating a military agreement. He argued that without a military agreement, the political agreement would be an "empty declaration."

On July 17, Molotov announced that instead of a political agreement and a military agreement, there must be only one agreement: political-military. Unless the British and French government agreed that the political and military parts of the agreement should form one indivisible whole, it would be pointless to continue the negotiations. When asked directly, both diplomats thought their governments would be prepared to commence military conversations. A week later, Molotov proposed Moscow as the site for the military conversations.

Back in London, Chamberlain was in no haste to conclude an alliance. He was still skeptical of the value of the aid that the Soviet Union could provide. In a crisis, he thought that the British and the French could not depend upon the Soviet Union. If the British and French governments obtained an agreement with the Soviet Union, he would not consider it a triumph because he did not value Soviet military ability very highly. In his mind, an agreement with the Soviet government amounted to a return to the pre-1914 alliance system. At one point, he had remarked that he really preferred to resign than sign an alliance with the Soviet Union. However, there was pressure from the House of Commons, as well as from the cabinet to reach an agreement with the Soviet government. Public Opinion polls strongly favored an alliance. Even among the Chiefs of Staff there had been a change of opinion, and now they looked favorably upon an alliance. As the pressure increased, Chamberlain conceded. On July 25 Halifax instructed Seeds to inform Molotov that the British government was prepared to commence military conversations in Moscow immediately without waiting for the completion of the alliance. The French government was also in agreement.

In contrast to Chamberlain's reluctance to conclude an agreement with the Soviet government, the reverse was the case with the French government. Bonnet and Daladier so dreaded a possible breakdown in the negotiations that early in the discussions they urged London to accept Molotov's terms. They argued that the collapse of the negotiations would only encourage Hitler in his plans and give the impression that the western powers could not organize an effective coalition. It was better to accept the Soviet terms than risk a breakdown in the negotiations. The French leaders feared the terrible consequences of if they rejected Molotov's demands.

Both the British and French governments had accepted Molotov's proposal for the military talks to be held in Moscow. Consequently it would be expected that high-ranking officials would represent the governments. In contrast to his eagerness to fly to Germany and meet with Hitler, Chamberlain had no wish to fly to Moscow for these high-level negotiations, and he objected to any other British politician going to Moscow. Winston Churchill and Anthony Eden had both volunteered to make the trip to Moscow.

With the possibility of war on the horizon, no high-ranking British general was interested in heading a delegation to negotiate a military agreement. Instead Admiral Sir Reginald Plunket-Ernle-Erle Drax, whose name sounded like a character in a Gilbert and Sullivan opera, was chosen to head the British delegation in which both the Royal Air Force and the Royal Navy would also be represented. Despite his name, Drax was a competent, intelligent officer who had been the first head of the Royal Naval Staff College and the principal naval aide to King George VI.

Before his departure, in a final conference with Halifax, Drax asked what he should do if the negotiations were to fail. Should there be a quick end to it or a slow withdrawal? If that were the case, Halifax instructed Drax to draw the negotiations out as long as possible. The British delegation was also instructed to avoid revealing any military information because London suspected possible Soviet-German collusion.

To head their delegation, the French chose General Joseph Doumenc, then commander of the first Military Region. Neither Drax nor Doumenc had as high a rank as did the head of the Soviet military delegation, Marshal Kliment Voroshilov, the Soviet defense minister.

A new problem arose. How would the Anglo-French delegations, which each numbered about twenty, travel to Moscow? Travel by rail across Nazi Germany to Moscow did not seem prudent. The use of British cruisers and destroyers to transport the delegations across the Baltic Sea was vetoed because it would appear too provocative. Air travel was too risky because fuel limitations meant a landing on German soil to refuel. Neither Britain nor France had a commercial airline with regular flights to Moscow. Bombers would be provocative as well as uncomfortable for the passengers. The method chosen was via a chartered merchant ship with a speed of thirteen knots, which took five days to make the journey to Leningrad where the delegation missed the train to Moscow. The delegation finally arrived in Moscow on August 11.

The first meeting on August 12 got off to an unpleasant start when the Soviet delegates produced a document appointing them as plenipotentiaries with authorization to sign. General Doumenc had authority to negotiate but not to sign. As for Drax, he had no written credentials whatsoever. He could only ask London to send them by air mail. They arrived on August 21, and by then it was too late.

The next problem arose when Voroshilov insisted on each delegation revealing the strength of their military forces and their plans to deal with the German threat. The British and French delegations were shocked because they had never planned to reveal such information. So they exaggerated the strength of their forces as did the Soviet delegation.

The question which ultimately wrecked the conference came up on August 13 when Voroshilov asked if Poland were to be attacked by Germany, would Soviet troops be allowed on Polish soil to fight German forces? Would Rumania, if attacked by Germany, permit Soviet forces to move across Rumanian territory? Voroshilov wanted a definite answer. Drax and Doumenc referred the problem to Paris and London. Drax could not expect any advice from London because Parliament was not in session, and Chamberlain and Halifax were not in London. The former had gone fishing, while the other was out was hunting. When the problem was presented to Colonel Beck in Warsaw, he refused to permit the passage of Soviet troops across Poland knowing that the unity of Poland would not long survive a Russian occupation.

The Soviet delegation, Drax complained, referred to the British and French governments as the "yielding powers," and presented their delegations with the Russian "demands (not requests) . . . somewhat in the manner of a victorious power dictating terms to a broken enemy."[15] They made evident their opinion that the British and French delegations had come as supplicants. In addition, they demanded that the British and French governments send a naval force into the Baltic and arrange with the Baltic states for naval bases for the Soviet fleet.

Voroshilov castigated the British and French governments for failing to give their delegations plenipotentiary power, while he did not really possess such power either. Whenever a definite decision was needed, he had to recess the meeting and hurry away to confer with Stalin. On August 17, Voroshilov adjourned the conference temporarily until the British and French delegations could obtain answers from their governments to the "cardinal question": would Soviet troops be permitted to pass through Poland and Rumania to make contact with enemy troops? Without this concession, Voroshilov declared, the Soviet Union could give no help to Britain and France. (In the political negotiations, Litvinov and Molotov had both neglected to bring up this "cardinal question," which Voroshilov now considered essential to any military negotiations.) While the British and French delegations were still consulting their governments, Voroshilov postponed the meetings indefinitely on August 21, with the excuse that the Soviet generals had to be with their troops on maneuvers. The meetings were never resumed, although on August 22 the French government instructed Doumenc to sign whatever terms he could get for a military convention that would include agreement to the passage of Soviet troops through Poland after the outbreak of war. Voroshilov refused further discussion, using the excuse that the British and Polish troops had not given their consent to the passage of troops.

Chamberlain abhorred the idea of an alliance because it would divide Europe. He had no wish to have Britain drawn into a war of Stalin's devising. Nor did he want Britain to go to war because Hitler had attacked the Soviet Union. He was unwilling to send Halifax or the chiefs of staff to Moscow for the negotiations. Likewise, Stalin was unwilling to dispatch Molotov or Voroshilov to London. With war on the horizon, ought not Britain and France have done whatever might have been necessary in order to reach an agreement on an alliance with the Soviet government? Not only was Chamberlain shortsighted, so were Stalin and Daladier.

Stalin and Molotov imagined that Britain was so in need of Soviet aid that the government would join the alliance no matter what the terms. However, Chamberlain never really desired an alliance with the Soviet Union. Instead he chose a policy of delay hoping that Hitler would come to his senses and postpone war. Despite the threat of war, nothing impelled Chamberlain to plunge ahead and conclude an alliance with the Soviet government as soon as possible. Instead, forced by Parliament and the cabinet, Chamberlain had reluctantly entered into negotiations with Stalin. The delays, the slow journey to the Soviet Union, the lack of credentials for their representatives, and the rank of the delegations all signaled to Moscow that Chamberlain's heart was not in these negotiations. Daladier and Bonnet lacked the gumption as well as will power to demand that Chamberlain change his policy concerning an alliance.

Stalin would make the same mistake as the British and French at Munich because he believed that he could avoid confrontation with Hitler. Nothing at that time indicated that the British and French governments would change their attitude and become resolute in their determination to stop Hitler. However, in August 1939, as Germany kept pressing, it seemed to Stalin that the better deal was to come to terms with Hitler, avoid war and leave Britain and France to their fate. In August 1939, Britain and France did not appear to Stalin to be a winning team. But in the end they were all at fault: Chamberlain, Halifax, Daladier, Bonnet, Molotov and Stalin: because they all abandoned the policy of collective security, Europe would have to pay the price. Had the three governments feared Hitler as much in 1939 as they were to fear him later, agreement might have been reached; but, as long as neither side believed Hitler to be dangerous enough to force a burial of their differences, agreement was impossible. Most important to remember, for the U.S.S.R. the more attractive offer—peace rather than war—was to come from Berlin.

Some weeks earlier, Berlin began a subtle campaign to woo the Soviet government away from Britain and France. Karl Schnurre, German trade negotiator, informed Georgi Astakov, the Soviet chargé d'affaires in Berlin on May 5 that Soviet contracts with the Skoda arms factory in the former Czechoslovakia would be honored. They next met on May 17. Then according to Astakov's report Schnurre brought up the subject of improving Nazi-Soviet relations. Astakov commented that an improvement in relations was possible if Germany so desired. If we are to believe Schnurre's report, Astakov "stated in detail that there were no conflicts in foreign policy between Germany and the Soviet Union and therefore there was no reason for any enmity between the two countries."[16] Astakov, declared, according to his report, that an improvement in relations between the two nations was possible if Germany so desired. Apparently Berlin was impressed by this exchange.

On May 30, State Secretary Ernst von Weizsaecker asked Astakov to call at the German Foreign Ministry, ostensibly to discuss a problem dealing with the Soviet Trade Delegation in Prague. Soon Weizsaecker shifted the discussion to Soviet-German relations, observing that normalization of relations had been obstructed by "rubble" which "some people wanted to pile even higher." He insisted that Moscow cease from claiming that between Germany and the Soviet Union there was an impenetrable wall of silence. Weizsaecker, the highest permanent official in the Germany Foreign Ministry, was speaking for the Fuehrer. The following day, in a speech before the supreme Soviet, Molotov not only accused Britain and France of trying to divert aggression towards the Soviet Union, but he indicated his government's lack of trust in these states. Molotov even hinted at the possibility of a resumption of economic negotiations with Germany.

At the same time, Moscow had a direct line to the German Foreign Ministry: a Soviet agent who was a high official in the German embassy in Warsaw. Stalin was consequently well informed concerning Hitler's plans to destroy Poland. By early May the agent disclosed that Germany planned to defeat Poland in a swift campaign and that preparations would be completed for action against Poland in July or August. If France and Britain intervened, Hitler was ready for a major war. By June Moscow learned that the attack on Poland was scheduled for late August or early September.

Limited negotiations continued between Berlin and Moscow. On June 14, although the two diplomats were barely acquainted, for no apparent reason Astakov paid a visit to the Bulgarian minister in Berlin, Parvan Dragonov. After a long talk stretching over two hours, Astakov announced: "If Germany would declare that she would not attack the Soviet Union or that she would conclude a non-aggression pact with her, the Soviet Union would probably refrain from concluding a treaty with England."[17] Was this evidence that Moscow wanted a deal while negotiating an alliance with Britain and France? Perhaps Astakov's account of the meeting does not bear this out, although he may merely have been testing the waters. Nevertheless, Dragonov, convinced that Astakov wanted his statement passed on to someone in the German Foreign Office, hurried to Ernest Woermann, a high official in the German Foreign Office, and reported this information.

Schulenberg, the German ambassador, went further on June 28 when he informed Molotov that a normalization of relations between Germany and the Soviet Union would be welcomed. Moreover, Germany would do all that it could to prove its good will towards the Soviet Union. Although Molotov admitted that the Soviet government desired good relations with all countries, Schulenberg sensed a strong distrust, based on Molotov's statements. Dissatisfied with the Soviet attitude, Hitler ordered a halt to any further talks.

Moscow, however, was still interested in maintaining some type of contact with Berlin. On July 18, the Soviet trade representative in Berlin, Evgeny Barbarin, appeared in the Foreign Ministry and announced to Schnurre that the Soviet government desired to discuss expanding German-Soviet economic relations. He even talked about signing a trade treaty. Ribbentrop was so excited by this report that he immediately selected Schnurre to take the first step towards a deal with the Soviet government. Ribbentrop, keeping the Foreign Ministry hierarchy in the dark as well as ambassador Schulenberg, ordered Schnurre to fly to Salzburg where the foreign minister had one of his many estates. There Ribbentrop, after instructing Schnurre in what he was to do and to say, directed him to return to Berlin and to keep his instructions secret.

As ordered by Ribbentrop, a meeting between Schnurre and Astakov was arranged for the evening of July 26 in a small, quiet room in Ewest's, a long-established Berlin restaurant, often used by German officials. It had a well-deserved reputation for providing privacy. For their protection, Schnurre and Astakov each brought along witnesses to their discussion. After a quiet dinner, with brandy and fine cigars, which lasted until 2:30 A.M., Schnurre went all out, proposing collaboration in economic matters and improvements in political relations. Astakov observed that restoring friendly relations would be a slow, gradual process. The Soviet Union felt threatened by Nazi foreign policy, even encircled. Schnurre declared that there was no threat against the Soviet Union. Britain was the target of Nazi foreign policy. Britain could offer nothing but a war and German hostility. Schnurre claimed that Germany, Italy, and the Soviet Union had one thing in common: their opposition to the capitalist democracies.

Astakov came away from the dinner meeting convinced that Germany was ready to come to an understanding with the Soviet government on all of the questions that were of concern to both sides and even to give security guarantees. Molotov, however, wanted more than talk, but he appeared interested in what the Germans were saying. As for Ribbentrop and Hitler, they were both delighted by the report of Astakov's reactions. Consequently, Ribbentrop ordered Schulenburg to present the same proposals to Molotov.

When Astakov dropped by the German Foreign Ministry on August 2, he was only interested in talking about the economic negotiations, but Ribbentrop could not resist inviting him in for a chat. Soon the foreign minister got to the point. Germany was favorably disposed towards Moscow. Ribbentrop stated: "There was no problem from the Baltic to the Black Sea that could not be solved between the two of us. . . . In case of Polish provocation [Germany] would settle accounts with Poland in the space of a week."[18] Ribbentrop indicated that he would be prepared as soon as the Soviet government indicated a desire to remold their relations.

After the restaurant meeting in Berlin, Schulenberg had received instructions to seek an appointment with Molotov as soon as possible, but he was unable to see him until August 3. The ambassador repeated Ribbentrop's declaration that no difference existed between the two nations from the Baltic to the Black Sea. Germany was prepared to come to an understanding with the Soviet Union on the matter of Poland. The German demands on Poland would not harm Soviet interests. Molotov thought the prospects for reaching an economic agreement were quite favorable. His government wanted to normalize and improve relations. Schulenberg believed that his comments had impressed Molotov; however, he thought the Soviet government was determined to conclude an agreement with Britain and France if they could fulfill Soviet wishes.

On August 10, when Astakov came to the Foreign Ministry to discuss an agricultural exhibition to be held in Moscow, Schnurre used the opportunity to express his government's desire to improve German-Soviet relations. The German government wished to know Molotov's attitude regarding Soviet interests. As for Poland, they hoped the Poles would see reason, but failing that matters would be solved by war. Moreover, his government could not believe that Moscow would take sides with the British. The upcoming military negotiations could take the form of an alliance against Germany.

Two days later, Astakov returned with a message from Moscow. The Soviet government was interested in discussing a variety of questions including Poland, but the discussion had to proceed by degrees. Moscow was proposed as the site for the negotiations. A delighted Ribbentrop, ordered Schulenburg to arrange for an interview with Molotov and to read a written statement to the Soviet foreign minister. If possible, Schulenberg should request an audience with Stalin to deliver this important message.

Hitler, however, had a troubled ally: Mussolini. Ciano had been dispatched to Germany to meet with Ribbentrop and Hitler. Worried over the impending war, which Mussolini dreaded, Ciano had been instructed to discuss ways of avoiding war because Duce feared that a war over Poland could escalate into a world war. Ciano found Hitler determined and very frank about his intentions. "Poland's whole attitude made it plain that in any conflict she would always be on the side of the opponents of Germany and Italy, her speedy liquidation could only be an advantage at the present moment in the inevitable clash with the western democracies."[19] Too many German divisions would have to be tied up watching Poland. But, Hitler assured Ciano, there was no immediate danger of world war; the western democracies would not be willing to commit themselves to anything so drastic. Hitler had decided that a showdown with Poland was essential, and that it would be up to Poland to decide whether or not fighting would occur. To Ciano's dismay, not only had Hitler decided upon a showdown, but it would be an immediate one. He would give Poland until August 31 to surrender because any military campaign launched after that date might run over into the rainy season, which usually began in the middle of October. Even more dismayed than when he had arrived, Ciano returned to Rome cursing Hitler for betraying Italy.

A confident Hitler reviewed the political situation with his generals on August 14. He again discounted the possibility of Britain engaging in a war over Poland. Furthermore, he announced, Britain lacked leadership. "The men I got to know in Munich are not the kind that start a new world war." He was confident that France was uninterested in the events in eastern Europe, that Russia would stay out of the war, and that, without leadership, other European nations would seek neutrality. He knew that the Anglo-French military forces were unprepared to face the armies of the new Germany. From tapped telephone conversations, he also knew that the British had been paving the way for him by trying to dampen the Poles' spirit. Already, he claimed, the British had put out feelers on his intentions for

Europe after he had disposed of Poland. He expected Britain to make a show of resistance to "talk big, even recall her ambassador, perhaps put a complete embargo on trade, [but] she is sure not to resort to armed intervention in the conflict."[20]

Time was growing short. The Anglo-French military delegation was already in Moscow engaged in negotiations when Schulenberg delivered Ribbentrop's message to Molotov on August 15. No conflict of interests remained between Germany and the Soviet Union. No problem existed between the Baltic and the Black Sea which both countries could not settle to their complete satisfaction. By concluding a military alliance, Britain and France were attempting to drive the Soviet Union into a war against Germany. Ribbentrop was prepared to visit Moscow, explain Hitler's views to Stalin and lay the foundations for a final settlement of German-Russian relations.

Stalin and Molotov now had to formulate a new strategy as the negotiations over a triple alliance with Britain and France were nearing collapse. Stalin's worst fear was a war with Germany while Britain and France remained inactive. It was necessary to devise a new policy involving Nazi Germany. Consequently, Molotov had questions which needed to be discussed. Would Germany be willing to conclude a nonaggression pact? Hitler consented. How did he feel about a joint guarantee of the Baltic states? Hitler was willing. Would he use German influence to persuade Japan to improve relations with Russia? Again, yes. But Molotov wanted Germany to sign an economic agreement. With no other choice if his military schedule were to be met, Hitler obliged.

At 2 A.M. on August 20, German and Soviet negotiators signed a trade agreement by which the Russians were to receive a credit of 200 million Reichsmarks and were to supply the Germans with a credit of 200 million Reichsmarks' worth of raw materials during the following two-year period. The way seemed clear for a political agreement. Ribbentrop wanted to come to Moscow immediately but Molotov insisted that the visit to complete the bargain should come a week later. That would mean a week's delay in Hitler's timetable. Consequently, Hitler had to resort to a personal message to Stalin in order to extract an invitation for Ribbentrop to come to Moscow sooner.

Ribbentrop flew into Moscow on August 23, and that afternoon he met Molotov and Stalin in the Kremlin. It did not take long for both sides to settle the wording and agree on a Non-Aggression Pact. The signing was followed by a splendid supper with plenty of vodka and numerous toasts. Stalin toasted the absent Hitler; then Ribbentrop toasted Stalin, the Soviet government, and good relations between the Soviet Union and Germany. Stalin and Ribbentrop toasted the Non-Aggression Pact and the new era of good relations between Germany and the Soviet Union. It was a wonderful evening for Ribbentrop. The embassy staff cheered him upon his return to the embassy and Hitler congratulated him by telephone when he learned of the successful negotiation of a Non-Aggression Pact.

The pact, which was to run for ten years, went into effect as soon as it had been signed. If one partner went to war, the other promised to remain neutral. Significantly, there was no escape clause automatically invalidating the pact if one member should launch an aggressive war. Thus, Stalin left Hitler free to attack Poland whenever he wished. A secret protocol, drafted in Moscow and accepted by Hitler, clinched the deal for Stalin: while Lithuania would belong in the German sphere of influence, Finland, Estonia, and Latvia would be in the Russian sphere; and Poland would be divided between Russia and Germany along the Narev, Vistula, and San Rivers. Germany would recognize Russian interest in Bessarabia (then in Rumania), and would claim no part of southeastern Europe. While Britain and France had sought to protect the independence of the small eastern European states that had emerged after World War I, Germany and the Soviet Union had now negotiated a pact to end their independence.

Hitler could now be certain that Stalin would not trouble him in the east while he attacked Poland and then turned his attention to Britain and France; and Stalin not only had peace but a promise of spheres of influence that Britain and France had denied him. (However, when the secret protocol was introduced in the Nuremberg trails, Soviet lawyers would denounce it as a forgery.)

Secure that the pact was to be signed the following day, Hitler called his senior commanders to an all-day conference on August

22 and announced to them that war with Poland must come in 1939, rather than later when conditions for war might not be so favorable for Germany. Now its enemies were unprepared for war. "There is no real armament in England, but only propaganda." France, short of troops because of the declining birthrate, had done little to rearm. The most that could be expected from the West at this time would be a blockade of Germany, which would be ineffective, or an attack mounted from the Maginot Line, which was impossible, according to Hitler. "Now Poland is in the position in which I wanted her," Hitler gloated. "Our enemies are small fry. I saw them in Munich." In another speech that same day, Hitler exhorted his officers to wage a brutal, relentless war, with the objective: "The wholesale destruction of Poland."[21]

This was not the speech of a ruler who would consider pulling back from war at the last moment. Hitler had committed himself and Germany without reservation. Peace was no longer possible unless Poland capitulated. He could not turn back without endangering his regime, because the German officer corps had no scruples about a war with Poland. The next day, he ordered war to begin on August 26 at 4:30 A.M.

Chamberlain continued to keep channels open to Berlin because he preferred a settlement to a war, but he dared not repeat his trips of the previous year even though hints had come from Berlin for a visit. Instead, having received reports that Hitler would begin his war on Poland between August 25 and 28, Chamberlain, at the suggestion of Halifax, resorted to a secret letter, sent to Hitler on August 22, attempting to convince Hitler that Britain would fight if German soldiers entered Poland.

In his letter, Chamberlain vowed that, despite the Nazi-Soviet pact, Britain would not step down from its obligations to Poland. Believing that war could have been avoided in 1914 if Britain had made its position clear, Chamberlain pointed out to Hitler that war between Britain and Germany would be a great calamity, and that there was nothing between Poland and Germany that could not be settled peacefully. He recommended a truce on both sides in order to settle minority problems, after which direct Polish-German discussions could begin.

When Neville Henderson, the British ambassador, presented the letter to Hitler on August 23, the Fuehrer went into one of his fits of rage. The British were preventing a settlement of the Polish question and preparing for war, he insisted, while Germany was only trying to defend itself. Thousands of Germans were being dragged off to Polish concentration camps, and the British had given the Poles a blank check for attacking Germany. The British would have to pay for this, he warned. He would not allow Germans to be slaughtered just to satisfy the whims of the British. If Poland made the slightest move against the Germans or against Danzig, Hitler intended to "intervene."

Later that day, Hitler handed Henderson a letter in which he swore that he had not sought any conflict with Britain, but that Danzig and the Corridor belonged in the German sphere of interest. Germany was prepared to settle these questions through negotiations, but the British pledge to Poland, coupled with allegations about German mobilization and German designs on other countries, had destroyed any Polish inclination to negotiate. Encouraged by the British, he insisted, the Poles had loosed a wave of terrorism against the Germans living in Poland, and Hitler would not tolerate these or further acts of provocation. Finally, if Britain and France carried out mobilization measures, he threatened to order the immediate mobilization of the Wehrmacht.

Unsaid but understood in Hitler's letter was the question, "Why fight for Poland?" He was striving to frighten the British—and thereby the French—away from Poland; but London did not retreat. On August 24, Parliament assembled and heard declarations from Chamberlain and Halifax that the government would stand by Poland. That same day, Parliament voted an emergency powers bill giving the executive exceptional powers to take whatever steps were necessary in the event of war. Apparently the news of the Nazi-Soviet pact had not been awesome enough to alter the government's policies, so Hitler would have to do more to bring the British to desert Poland.

Hitler summoned Henderson to the Reichschancellery on August 25 and gave him an offer intended to be as decisive as that given Russia. Hitler indicated that he was prepared to make another offer to Britain after the German-Polish problem had been solved. He was willing to conclude an agreement that would "not only guarantee the existence of the British empire in all circumstances as far as Germany is concerned but would also if necessary assure the British empire of German assistance."[22] He claimed to be ready to accept a limitation on armaments and to be uninterested in altering the western frontiers of Germany.

Hitler also gave a "Why fight for Poland?" message to French Ambassador Robert Coulondre. The possibility that Germans and French should spill their blood over Poles was dreadful; but Germany could not tolerate the Polish provocations much longer. Seventy thousand refugees had been forced to flee Poland; on the 24th, seven Germans had been shot; thirty German reservists had been machine-gunned; and Polish ships had fired on a German plane carrying a state secretary. Hitler implored the ambassador to give his message to Daladier quickly. He said: "I want to avoid a conflict. I will not attack France, but if she enters the war, I will carry on to the end."[23]

Later in the same day, Hitler telephoned Mussolini to tell him that an attack on Poland was imminent and that he needed the help that Mussolini had promised in the Pact of Steel. Faced with the message he had been dreading and with his armies not yet recovered from the Spanish Civil War, Mussolini had to yield to the pleading of Ciano and confess to Hitler that Italy could not go to war unless it was furnished with urgently needed supplies.

Before receiving Mussolini's reply, Hitler confidently ordered the attack of Poland to begin the next day, August 26. Then, about 4:30 A.M., the news reached Berlin that Britain and Poland had joined in an alliance, promising to support each other if attacked by an aggressor; in secret clauses, they indicated that Germany was the anticipated aggressor and that a threat to Danzig would be cause enough for invoking the alliance. Then came Mussolini's message that Italy would not come to his aid, destroying Hitler's hope that the Italian fleet would keep the British occupied in the Mediterranean. Hitler's confidence was badly shaken. About 7:30 P.M., he canceled the order for war.

Hitler's decision resulted more from the Anglo-Polish alliance than from Mussolini's defection, because the alliance appeared to be a direct challenge. However, for the Chamberlain government, it was only another effort to shock Hitler into negotiating over Poland and to remove any doubts about Britain's position. For Hitler it meant that he must devote more time to isolating Poland from its new ally.

Early in the morning of August 27, Hitler was roused from his bed by Goering with the news that a Swedish businessman, Birger Dahlerus, who had acted as an intermediary between London and Berlin before, had brought a message from Halifax. Dahlerus reported that the British government needed time to consult with Henderson and to draft a reply to Hitler's latest proposal and that it was interested in solving the question that troubled the peace of Europe. Hitler replied with a rambling monologue on his early career and his troubles with the British. Then he questioned Dahlerus on life in Britain. Finally, Hitler stated his terms—Danzig and the Corridor, a guarantee of rights for the Germans living in Poland, a German guarantee of the Polish frontiers, return of the German colonies, and a pledge to defend the British Empire. Furthermore, he insisted, he must have a conference with British leaders, hinting at another Munich.

With patience, Hitler could have reached his goal. When Chamberlain received Dahlerus' report, he seriously considered the possibilities; he doubted if the Poles would be willing to concede all of the Corridor. At this time, Chamberlain would have accepted the return of Danzig to Germany and the formation of an extraterritorial road across the Corridor, which were the original demands presented by Ribbentrop in October 1938. Having worn down the British to this point in less than a year, it is likely that, if Hitler had waited, he could have obtained all his objectives this way.

His campaign to frighten the French brought a doleful message from Daladier on August 26. The premier assured Hitler that German-Polish differences could be settled peacefully; but he warned that, if there were a war bloodier than the last, the only victors would be the "forces of destruction and barbarism."[24] Hitler replied on August 27 with the accustomed story of the iniquitous Treaty of Versailles and with a repetition of his demand for Danzig and the Corridor. To his message, he added a prophecy: if war should come, whatever the outcome, "the Polish state of today would disappear in one way or another."[25]

By August 28, Hitler had developed a policy that he hoped would isolate Poland in time for the war, which was now planned for September 1. With the intention of driving a wedge between the British and the Poles, he would force Poland into an unfavorable position through demands for Danzig, the Corridor, and a plebiscite. If he could get the British to accept his offer and the Poles to reject it, then he would have his war only with Poland. By now, however, the pressures had begun to take their toll on Hitler; one of his aides reported him "exhausted, haggard, croaking voice, preoccupied."[26]

About 10:30 A.M. on August 28, Henderson, "fortified by a half bottle of champagne,"[27] brought Chamberlain's message to Hitler. The Prime Minister recommended a settlement between Poland and Germany, to be guaranteed by other powers and to be undertaken by direct negotiations between Poland and Germany. He assured the Fuehrer that Beck was prepared to enter into such discussions. However, Beck's promise had not been secured without pressure. By August 29, Polish prospects were far from promising. German troops were moving into position along the Polish frontiers, and there were stories of Russian troop movements on the eastern borders of Poland. Rumors circulated about German units entering Slovakia. Beck wanted to proceed with general mobilization, but Sir Howard Kennard, the British ambassador, talked him into postponing it until London could receive Hitler's reply.

That evening about 7:15 P.M., Henderson reported to the Reichschancellery, where he received a memorandum containing Hitler's response. After listing his complaints over the conduct of the Poles, which had finally forced him to safeguard German national interests, he announced that he was willing to accept the British proposal for direct negotiations if a Polish emissary was in Berlin by August 30 with full powers to negotiate. Hitler planned to use the tactics that had been so successful with Schuschnigg and Hacha: get one person into a position to make the decision, and then bully and threaten him until he would surrender his country entirely.

In passing Hitler's proposal on to Lipski, Henderson begged that it be accepted. Beck, he thought, would be just the one for the trip. However, remembering the examples of Schuschnigg and Hacha, the Polish government withstood the pleas. They preferred to fight rather than send Beck, or any other representative, to have to confront Hitler's bullying. On the morning of August 30, Poland ordered a general mobilization.

One delay after another prevented Henderson from conveying London's reply to Ribbentrop until about midnight on August 30. Henderson reported that Warsaw had been informed of Hitler's request, but the first step for any negotiation would have to be for Germany and Poland themselves to work out the arrangements. The British government found it impossible to have an emissary with the powers requested in Berlin as soon as August 30. In the meantime, some temporary arrangements should be worked out to try to ease the tensions. Henderson suggested that it might be helpful for Germany to follow the normal procedure of talking directly with the Polish ambassador and having him convey the German terms to Warsaw.

Almost as if he had not heard Henderson at all, Ribbentrop whipped out a document and proceeded to rattle off sixteen points demanded by Hitler. Henderson asked for a copy but Ribbentrop refused, explaining that, because the time limit for a Polish emissary to appear in Berlin had expired, the proposals were useless. Interpreting this as an ultimatum, the usually obsequious Henderson angrily turned on Ribbentrop. The argument between the two men became so heated that observers feared they might come to blows.

Ribbentrop was merely following orders. If he had handed Henderson a copy of the conditions, they could have become the basis for negotiations leading to a call for an international conference similar to that at Munich in 1938. Hitler had no wish to have another Munich Conference where someone could arrange a compromise and block the outbreak of war. To prevent such an occurrence, earlier in the summer, he had ordered the German ambassadors in London and Warsaw recalled home and forbidden to return to their posts. Hitler said that he did not want some "Schweinhund" (SOB) presenting a compromise that might prevent the outbreak of war with Poland.[28]

The terms read off by Ribbentrop were deceptively liberal. Danzig would be returned to Germany, but the fate of the Corridor would be determined by plebiscite conducted by an international commission. All Polish forces would have to evacuate the area immediately, but there should be a year's delay in the plebiscite (which would give the Nazis time to establish their hold on the area). Were Poland to win the plebiscite, Germany would have to be given an extraterritorial traffic zone across the Corridor. If Germany won, Poland would receive a similar right of access to the sea. Also, if the Corridor returned to Germany, an exchange of populations would be arranged to alleviate the minority problem; and an international commission would be created to examine all minority complaints, with both countries compensating for any damages. Both nations would enter into binding agreements to protect the minorities residing within their frontiers. And finally, once these agreements were accepted, Poland and Germany would demobilize their military forces.

Hitler hoped that the British would take the bait and the Poles would refuse it, thereby driving a wedge between Britain and Poland. He also intended that his proposals would serve as an alibi for the record—to make his case look good not only to the German people but to the rest of the world as well. Hitler, however, never wanted this document to become the basis for compromise, trapping him into another Munich Conference. Consequently the actual terms of the document were kept from the Poles and the British until after the "offer" had lapsed. In the evening of August 31, the terms were broadcast to the world as German soldiers took up their positions for the attack on Poland.

In the morning of August 31, Hitler issued the directive for war. In accordance with *Operation White*, hostilities would begin at 4:45 A.M. on September 1. Flights over neutral territory by the Luftwaffe were prohibited unless there were indications that large French and British formations were on the way, in which case the Luftwaffe would counter enemy air attacks. If Britain and France did attack, German forces would remain on the defensive to make Britain and France appear responsible for war.

Meanwhile, the negotiations continued. Henderson had been prodding the Polish ambassador into inquiring officially about Hitler's terms, and Goering made certain that the terms were given to Dahlerus, who of course passed them on to the British embassy and to the Polish ambassador. As Hitler had hoped, the pressure was now on the Poles. In the afternoon of August 31, Beck gave in to the pressure from London and Paris and instructed Lipski to announce to Ribbentrop that Poland would exchange views directly with Germany on arrangements for future discussions. But Lipski would not be empowered to accept any document himself or to discuss Hitler's proposals. At 6:30 in the evening, Lipski reported to Ribbentrop, who asked if Lipski had been given the power to negotiate. After receiving the negative reply and after reminding Lipski that Hitler had asked for an emissary with full powers by August 30, Ribbentrop curtly ended the interview. When Lipski returned to the embassy, he found that the telephone lines to Warsaw had been cut and he had no way of communicating with his government.

To reinforce his case that the war was defensive, Hitler staged incidents along the German-Polish frontiers. Germans dressed in Polish uniforms fired a few shots and placed bodies of Gestapo prisoners dressed in German uniforms along the border as evidence of a Polish attack. Another detachment of German soldiers dressed as Poles entered a German radio station near Gleiwitz and broadcast in Polish a report of the "attack" on Germany.

Now, having established his case carefully to make it appear that he was complying with the terms of the Paris peace pact, Hitler had his troops cross the Polish borders the next morning, right on schedule. With Poland invaded on three sides in broad daylight and with the planes of the Luftwaffe bombing towns and railroads, the peace negotiated on November 11, 1918, had ended.

As London and Paris digested the first reports of fighting in Poland on September 1, they wrestled with their reply to Hitler's aggression. Both governments had agreed that they should declare war jointly, but achieving that aim was not easy.

The British cabinet decided to warn Berlin that unless the German government suspended the invasion and prepared to promptly withdraw troops from Poland, the British government would fulfill the terms of the Anglo-Polish alliance. In Paris, because the French parliament had been summoned to meet on September 3, Bonnet rejected a time limit in any warning to Germany without Parliament's approval. For the same reason, he refused to allow the ambassadors to ask for their passports if the German reply was unsatisfactory. That evening Henderson delivered the warning to Ribbentrop, who was unusually polite but who also accused the Poles of provocation by invading Germany. One hour later, the French ambassador delivered a similar warning to Ribbentrop.

On September 2, Bonnet asked London for a forty-eight hour time limit after the issuance of any ultimatum because the general staff needed the time for mobilization. If that was not enough, the Italian government suggested an armistice followed by a five-power conference. Bonnet eagerly accepted it, even though German troops would still remain on Polish soil. The British cabinet, after much debate, decided that Chamberlain and Halifax could work out the communication with the French. That evening, after consulting with Daladier on his statement, Chamberlain went before the House of Commons without an ultimatum, a time limit, or any promise of aid to Poland. He admitted that as yet there was no agreement with the French. He announced only that if Germany merely agreed to withdraw troops from Poland (which was not the same as actually completing a withdrawal), then the government would consider that affairs were back to the status of August 31, before the invasion. Then Britain would be prepared to join in a conference on the PolishGerman problem. When angry members on both sides of the House of Commons condemned the government's inaction, a shocked Prime Minister promised a definite statement the next day. Before the night was over, the Chamberlain government almost collapsed when rebellious cabinet members went on a "sit-down strike" until the Prime Minister agreed to an ultimatum with a two-hour time limit. At 9:00 A.M. on September 3, Henderson delivered an ultimatum with such a time limit. When no response came from Berlin at 11:00 A.M. to the ultimatum that the invasion be halted, Britain went to war. France followed at 5:00 P.M. Both countries were in a conflict they had never wanted and had labored to avoid. However, Hitler had been determined to have a war over Poland. Now he had it, although he had not wished to fight Britain and France at the same time.

CONCLUSION

War came to Europe in 1939 when Hitler failed to turn Poland into a vassal state. Since Poland had rejected his demands, the alternative for him was war; he would not be cheated out of this war as he had been at Munich. Hitler must assume chief responsibility for the war of September 1939. He did not stumble into war with Poland by mistake. Instead, he ordered his generals to carry out the pledge that he had made to them on February 3, 1933, to use Germany's power to seize living space.

To the German public, however, Hitler had promised to regain lost German territory and to restore his country to its rightful place in the world. Poland had received German territory through the Treaty of Versailles, the document that Hitler had pledged to revoke. This argument for persecuted German minorities was one that he relied on to dissuade the British and French from fighting for Poland. Why die for an injustice created by the detested Treaty of Versailles? But the treaty powers were willing to pay only so much and no more for peace.

After Hitler achieved *Anschluss* with Austria, the balance of power shifted in Germany's favor; it shifted even more when Czechoslovakia fell. But the appeasers no longer felt as generous as they had in the past. After Munich, appeasement was on its way out. Hitler, feeling overconfident from his victory, did not realize that Britain and France were capable of any other policy but appeasement, and so he believed that he could take Poland without any interference. Hitler could not understand that events since September 1938 had so shaken British politicians that there had been a revolution in British policy. Tories, Liberals, and Laborites had finally resolved to go to war if necessary. Hitler not only had forced unity on British opinion, but he had driven the House of Commons to rebel against appeasement. As far as he could see, Britain and France could be counted on to respond to his takeover of Poland in the same way they had responded to the loss of Czechoslovakia. Chamberlain's offer of concessions presented through secret contacts in late August 1939 only confirmed Hitler's beliefs that the men of Munich would not stand up to him. It was his failing that he simply could not grasp the immense effect that the fall of Czechoslovakia had had on his foes. No longer would the British and French swallow his tales of mistreated German minorities. His claim that only Germans should be gathered into a greater Reich had been revealed as a hoax.

Since 1939 some historians have argued that, if nations had acted earlier, there would have been no war. If the League had fought Japan over Manchuria, they claim, or if the League had defended Ethiopia in 1935, then Hitler would not have attacked Poland. But it would have been impossible for Britain and France to participate in any kind of war—offensive or defensive, small-scale or large-scale—before 1939, because neither the people nor the governments of the two countries were conditioned to the idea of war. The only way they could accept war after 1938 was for it to be thrust upon them in a series of crises, such as those that finally culminated in the German invasion of Poland. Arguments over when and where Hitler should have been halted, then, are purely academic, because before September 1, 1939, Hitler had done nothing that any major power considered dangerous enough to warrant precipitating a general European war.

Until German troops invaded Poland, Hitler exploited the western powers' fears. They dreaded the outbreak of war—any war—in Europe. The possibility of a European conflict escalating into a general war similar to 1914–1918 drove the British government to seek the peaceful solution of volatile disputes in Europe. This fear of war had induced the British to accept Hitler's list of minority grievances, despite their cost, in order to save the peace in Europe. Moreover, the British even tried to achieve some form of a general settlement involving economic and colonial concessions in return for Germany's acceptance of the boundaries of post-1919 eastern Europe. Such a settlement was never Hitler's intention. He carefully avoided such diplomatic agreements, except for his error at Munich. But the Czechoslovak coup of March 15, 1939 revealed his insincerity and proved that a general settlement with Hitler was impossible.

France was even more fearful of war than Britain. Many short-lived French cabinets were filled with politicians who lacked statesmanship qualities and who were frequently involved in parliamentary intrigues. Because the French remembered the terrible casualties their country had suffered in the 1914–1918 war, they regarded any concessions as better than another bloodbath. Fatalistically, they envisioned either a future war that would destroy France as a great power or the acceptance of German preponderance in Europe. They realized that France could not stand alone in Europe but depended on an alliance with Britain. In the spring of 1939, their ally could offer only two combat-ready divisions. French generals, whose estimates of German military strength bordered on the fantastic, only increased the politicians' apprehensions; the generals actually frightened themselves. Without certainty of victory, they did not believe that France should fight Germany.

The greatest weakness of France was its lack of national unity. The rift between left and right was wider than ever by the summer of 1939, but if France were to play the role of a great power, the breach had to be closed. Yet it was not to be. Because of political divisions, the specter of hundreds of thousands of dead and wounded, the frightened, overage generals, and bitterly divided cabinets, France no longer had the strength to play the role of a great power.

France could expect little support from its ally, Soviet Russia, who was only too happy to watch the imperialist powers fight each other. Even when Germany threatened Poland, Stalin was eager to join in a deal with Germany to partition eastern Europe and divide Poland. Although Stalin knew that Hitler planned to turn on the West after destroying Poland, he nevertheless joined in the Non-Aggression Pact and in so doing encouraged Hitler to start the war.

For too long, appeasers had imagined that Hitler was seeking only to revise the hateful Treaty of Versailles. They could not grasp the truth: Hitler wanted a series of short wars that would be directed against the individual countries. In each case victory in one war would increase the likelihood of German victory in the next. For Hitler, the sooner the wars commenced the better, because Germany could lose its initial advantage in its readiness for war over other nations. In these campaigns, Hitler's goal would be *Lebensraum,* living space that would be seized from other states. The native populations, especially those of inferior racial stock, would be enslaved and either worked to death or deliberately exterminated. Ultimately, Germany would dominate Europe, but this goal was obtainable only through a series of limited wars.

But Hitler's plan for a series of separate wars collapsed in 1939 when Britain and France went to war, even though they had no intention of aiding Poland. The Nazi seizure of Norway and Denmark, the defeat of Holland, Belgium, and France seemed to indicate that perhaps Hitler's strategy might work after all. But, in 1940, the British spoiled his plan by refusing to admit defeat. Then Hitler erred by attacking the Soviet Union before conquering Britain. Because of Hitler's wars, Japan was emboldened to attack the United States, turning a European conflict into a global war. Hitler compounded his errors by declaring war on the United States. Thus Hitler's series of separate, limited wars had escalated into a global conflict.

It is of course true that Hitler had never anticipated the world war that developed from the Polish invasion. He had hoped for a short war that would be over so quickly that Britain and France would have to consider the conquest of Poland a fait accompli. He would then have time to plan for his next war in the West. It was a gamble, but Hitler was accustomed to gambling. He had wagered before when the odds were greater, and he had won. However, in September 1939, his gambling luck ran out, and the whole world would have to pay his debts.

NOTES

1 Bullitt to Hull, April 7, 1939, *Foreign Relations of the United States,* 1939, I, pp. 117–119.

2 Beck to Lipski, September 19, 1938, *Diplomat in Berlin, 1933–1939, Papers and Memoirs of Jozef Lipski* (New York, 1968), p. 406.

3 Neurath memorandum, January 14, 1938, *Documents on German Foreign Policy,* Series D, V, p. 39.

4 *Memorandum* by Hewel, October 24, 1938, ibid., pp. 105–106.

5 Halifax to Hoare, March 17, 1939, *Documents on British Foreign Policy,* Third Series, IV, p. 367.

6 Wohltat to Wiehl, February 27, 1939, *Documents on German Foreign Policy,* Series D, V, p. 407.

7 Keith Feiling, *Neville Chamberlain,* (London, 1946), p. 401.

8 Hitler's directive to the Commander-in-Chief of the Army, March 25, 1939, *Documents on German Foreign Policy,* Series D, VI, p. 117.

9 Halifax to Kennard, March 21, 1939, *Documents on British Foreign Policy,* Third Series, IV, p. 436.

10 Parliamentary Debates, House of Commons, Fifth Series, vol. 345, col. 2415.

11 Max Beloff, *The Foreign Policy of Soviet Russia, 1929– 1941,* Vol. 2, (Oxford , 1948), pp. 221–223.

12 Weizsaecker memorandum, April 17, 1939, *Documents on German Foreign Policy,* series D, Vol. VI, pp. 266–267.

13 Seeds to Halifax, May 28, 1939, *Documents on British Foreign Policy,* Third Series, V, p. 711.

14 Seeds to Halifax, May 30, ibid., p. 722

15 Drax to Chatfield, August 16, 1939, *Documents on British Foreign Policy,* Third Series, VII, p. 33.

16 Schnurre memorandum, May 17,1939, ibid.,p. 536

17 Woermann memorandum, ibid., pp. 728–729.

18 Ribbentrop to Schulenburg, August 3,1939, ibid., 1050.

19 Schmittt memorandum, August 12, 1939, ibid., p.42

20 Halder notebook, August 14,1939, ibid., p.555.

21 Memorandum on Hitler's speeches, August 22, 1939, in ibid., Series D, VII, pp. 200–206.

22 Hitler to Henderson, August 25, 1939, in ibid., p. 281.

23 Coulondre to Bonnet, August 25, 1939, *Le livre jaune français* (Paris, 1939), p. 313.

24 Daladier to Hitler, August 26, 1939, *Documents on German Foreign Policy*, Series D, VII, p. 331.

25 Hitler to Daladier, August 27, 1939, in ibid., p. 359.

26 Halder's notebook, August 28, 1939, in ibid., p. 564.

27 Henderson to Halifax, August 29, 1939, *Documents on British Foreign Policy*, Third Series, VII, p. 386.

28 Gerhard Weinberg, Germany, *Hitler and World War II: Essays in Modern German and World History* (Cambridge, 1995) p. 148.

BIBLIOGRAPHICAL ESSAY

Since the first edition of this book, the publication of documentary materials and the opening of archives have facilitated research on the origins of World War II. The new studies have enabled readers to obtain a better understanding of this important historical problem. Consequently I have limited the books listed in the bibliography chiefly to those published in the English language and included works in foreign languages only when there was no alternative in English.

The Royal Institute of International Affairs' *Survey of International Affairs* (London and New York, 1923–) provides a useful yearly account of events since 1920. During the war the series was halted but resumed in 1951, using newly published diplomatic documents. Beginning with the Czechoslovak Crisis, *1938*, vols. II–III (1951), *The World in March 1939* (1952), and *The Eve of the War, 1939* (1958) give an excellent survey of the eighteen months preceding the outbreak of the war.

The earliest controversial study of this problem was A. J. P. Taylor, *The Origins of the Second World War* (London, 1961, and subsequent American editions). Occasionally inaccurate but always interesting, Taylor's interpretations should be treated critically and balanced with more orthodox accounts. There are excellent analyses of Taylor's book in *The Origins of the Second World War Reconsidered: The A. J. P. Taylor Debate after Twenty Five Years,* edited by Gordon Martel (Boston, 1986) and *The Origins of the Second World War Reconsidered: A. J. P. Taylor and the Historians* (London, 1999), also edited by Gordon Martel. Other studies of the origins of World War II include Laurence Lafore, *The*

End of Glory: An Interpretation of the Origins of World War II (New York, 1970); W. Rogers Louis, ed., *The Origins of the Second World War: A. J. P. Taylor and His Critics* (New York, 1972); Joachim Remak, *The Origins of the Second World War* (Englewood Cliffs, N.J., 1976); Maurice Baumont, *The Origins of the Second World War* (New Haven, 1978); Anthony F. Adamthwaite, *The Making of the Second World War,* 2nd ed. (London, 1979); Esmonde Robertson, ed., *The Origins of the Second World War: Historical Interpretations* (London, 1971); and Hans W. Gatzke, ed., *European Diplomacy Between Two Wars, 1919–1939* (Chicago, 1972). More recently there is Martin Kitchen, *Europe Between the Wars: A Political History* (New York, 1988); and P. M. H. Bell, *The Origins of the Second World War in Europe* (New York, 1986). *Paths to War: New Essays on the Origins of the Second World War* (New York, 1989) edited by Robert Boyce and Esmonde M. Robertson, is useful. One of the best studies of international affairs before 1933 is Sally Marks, *The Illusion of Peace: International Relations in Europe, 1918–1933,* 2nd ed. (New York, 2000). Victor Rothwell, *Origins of the Second World War* (Manchester, U.K., 2001) examines the origins of World War II from the Versailles Treaty to Pearl Harbor. Richard and Andrew Wheatcroft, *The Road to War,* 2nd ed. (London, 1999) is important for the interwar period. For the Mediterranean, there is Reynolds M. Salerno, *Vital Crossroads: The Mediterranean Origins of the Second World War, 1935–1940* (Ithaca, 2002). For the nations in Eastern Europe there is Anita Prazmowska, *Eastern Europe and the Origins of the Second World War* (New York 2000). Michael Jabara Carley, *1939: The Alliance that Never Was and the Coming of World War II* (Chicago, 1999) is an important study based on archival materials. Williamson Murray *The Change in the European Balance of Power, 1938–1939: The Path to Ruin* (Princeton, 1984) is excellent. For a valuable analysis of the role of totalitarian dictatorships in the twentieth century read Bruce F. Pauley, *Hitler, Stalin, and Mussolini. Totalitarianism in the Twentieth Century,* 2nd ed. (Wheeling, Ill., 2003).

On the history of the peace treaties and the postwar problems, Paul Birdsall, *Versailles Twenty Years After* (New York, 1941) is a good but dated account of the writing of the Versailles Treaty. Ferdinand Czernin, *Versailles, 1919* (New York, 1961) contains a useful collection of documents on the Peace Conference and the Treaty. One of the best studies of the Peace Conference is Seth P. Tillman, *Anglo-American Relations at the Paris Peace Conference of 1919* (Princeton, 1961). Arno J. Mayer, *The Politics and Diplomacy of Peacemaking: Containment and Counterrevolution at Versailles 1918–1919* (New York, 1968) examines the forces which influenced the Paris Peace Conference. For the German side there is Alma Luckau, *The German Delegation at the Paris Peace Conference* (New York, 1941). A book which had a powerful impact, John Maynard Keynes's *Economic Consequences of the Peace* (New York, 1920) should be supplemented by Étienne Mantoux, *The Carthaginian Peace or the Economic Consequences of Mr. Keynes* (New York, 1952). More recent studies include Alan Sharp, *The Versailles Settlement: Peacemaking in Paris, 1919* (Basingstoke, U.K., 1991); and Margaret Owen, *Paris 1919: Six Months that Changed the World* (New York, 2002). *The Treaty of Versailles: A Reassessment after 75 years* (New York, 1998) edited by Man F. Boemeke, Gerald D. Feldman, and Elizabeth Glaser, is important. Robert H. Ferrell, *Peace in Their Time: The Origins of the Kellogg-Briand Peace Pact* (New Haven, 1952) is excellent, and so is Jon Jacobson, *Locarno Diplomacy: Germany and the West 1925–1929* (Princeton, 1972). Edward W. Bennett, *The Diplomacy of the Financial Crisis, 1931* (Cambridge, Mass., 1962) is important, as is his book *German Rearmament and the West, 1932–1933* (Princeton, 1979). On the League of Nations, the best study is F. P. Walters, *History of the League of Nations,* 2 vols. (New York, 1952). For Eastern Europe consult C. A. Macartney and A. A. Palmer, *Independent Eastern Europe* (New York, 1962). Gordon A. Craig and Felix Gilbert, *The Diplomats, 1919–1939,* 2 vols. (New York, 1963), is still the best work on diplomats and their professional activities.

For the history of Germany there is Gordon A. Craig, *Germany 1866–1945* (New York, 1978), and for a detailed account of the political history of the Weimar Republic read Erich Eyck, *A History of the Weimar Republic,* 2 vols. (Cambridge, Mass., 1962–1963). For the problems of German diplomacy there is Paul Seabury, *The Wilhelmstrasse* (Berkeley, 1954). On Stresemann, see Henry L. Bretton, *Stresemann and the Rearmament of Germany* (Baltimore, 1954); and Henry Ashby Turner, *Stresemann and the Politics of the Weimar Republic* (Princeton, 1963). The German army and its influence on foreign policy had long been studied in a number of books. These include Harold J. Gordon, *The Reichswehr and the German Republic 1919–1926* (Princeton, 1957); F. L. Carsten, *The Reichswehr and Politics, 1918–1933* (Oxford, 1966); John W. Wheeler Bennett, *The Nemesis of Power: The German Army in Politics, 1918–1945,* 2nd ed. (New York, 1964); Robert J. O'Neill, *The German Army and the Nazi Party, 1933–1939,* 2nd ed. (London, 1968); and Gaines Post, Jr., *The Civil-Military Fabric of Weimar Foreign Policy* (Princeton, 1973)

There are many books about Adolf Hitler. Alan Bullock, *Hitler: A Study in Tranny,* rev. ed. (New York, 1962) has become a classic. Joachim C. Fest, *Hitler* (New York, 1977) is an important biography. William Carr, *Hitler: A Study in Personality and Politics* (London, 1978) is fascinating look at Hitler's personality and his era. The most recent, detailed biography based on new sources is Ian Kershaw, *Hitler, 1889–1936: Hubris* (New York, 1999), and *Hitler, 1936–1945: Nemesis* (New York, 2000). Gerhard Weinberg, *Germany, Hitler and World War II: Essays in Modern German and World History* (Cambridge, U.K., 1995) is an important selection of essays dealing with German history in the twentieth century. Hitler's speeches are in Norman H. Baynes, ed., *The Speeches of Adolf Hitler, April 1922–August 1939,* 2 vols. (London, 1942). His comments and observations can be found in H. R. Trevor Roper, ed., *Hitler's Secret Conversations, 1941–1944* (New York, 1953), and his *The Testament of Adolf Hitler: The Hitler-Bormann Documents* (London, 1969). For Hitler's ideas before he came to power, read *Mein Kampf* (Boston, 1943) and *Hitler's Secret Book* (New York, 1961). Hermannn Rauschnigg, *The Voice of Destruction* (New York, 1940), is an important source for Hitler's ideas on foreign policy. For a history of Nazi Germany, there is the brilliant synthesis of Karl Dietrich Bracher, *The German Dictatorship: The Origins, Structure, and Effects of National Socialism* (New York, 1970). The most detailed and authoritative account of Hitler's foreign policy is Gerhard L. Weinberg, *The Foreign Policy of Hitler's Germany: Diplomatic Revolution in Europe, 1933–1939* (Chicago, 1973), and *The Foreign Policy of Hitler's Germany: Starting World War II, 1937–1939* (Chicago, 1980). One of the best works on Hitler's ideas about expansion is Eberhard Jackel, *Hitler's World View: A Blueprint for Power* (Cambridge, U.K., 1981). On Hitler's long-range goals see Klaus Hildebrand, *The*

Foreign Policy of the Third Reich (Berkeley, 1973), and Norman Rich, *Hitler's War Aims: Ideology, the Nazi State and the Course of Expansion,* 2 vols. (New York, 1973). Esmonde Robertson's *Hitler's Pre-War Policy and Military Plans, 1933–1939* (London, 1963) is enlightening. L. B. Namier, *Europe in Decay: A Study in Disintegration, 1936–1940* (New York, 1950), and *In the Nazi Era* (New York, 1952) are excellent critical analyses of documentary collections and memoirs.

For a useful survey of Italy under Mussolini, there is Alan Cassels, *Fascist Italy,* 2nd ed. (Arlington Heights, Ill., 1984). Gaetano Salvemini, *Prelude to World War II* (New York, 1954) stresses the role of Italy. Elizabeth Wiskemann, *The Rome-Berlin Axis: A History of Relations between Hitler and Mussolini* (New York, 1949) is still helpful but should be supplemented by Ivone Kirkpatrick, *Mussolini: A Study in Power* (New York, 1964). On Mussolini's foreign policy read Alan Cassels, *Mussolini's Early Diplomacy* (Princeton, 1970) and Esmonde M. Robertson, *Mussolini as Empire-Builder: Europe and Africa, 1932–1936* (London, 1977). For a detailed account of the origins of the struggle between Italy and Ethiopia, there is George W. Baer, *The Coming of the Italian-Ethiopian War* (Cambridge, Mass., 1967) and for its impact on the League of Nations see Baer's *Test Case: Italy, Ethiopia, and the League of Nations* (Stanford, 1976). For a balanced treatment there is Frank M. Hardie, *The Abyssinian Crisis* (London, 1974). Mario Toscano, *The Origins of the Pact of Steel* (Baltimore, 1967), is a classic study of this alliance.

For other international events, see Konrad Hugo Jarausch, *The Four Power Pact, 1933* (Madison, 1965), which is a thorough examination of this strange agreement. Hugh Thomas, *The Spanish Civil War* (New York, 1961), is the most comprehensive history of this conflict.

On the Austrian problem there is the authoritative study by Bruce F. Pauley, *Hitler and the Forgotten Nazis: A History of Austrian National Socialism* (Chapel Hill, 1981). Other books on the relations between Austria and Germany include Radomir Luza, *Austro-German Relations in the Anschluss Era* (Princeton, 1975) and Jurgen Gehl, *Austria, Germany and the Anschluss, 1931–1938* (London, 1963). On the Dollfuss murder, Walter B. Maass, *Assassination in Vienna* (New York 1972), is a dramatic account.

Gordon Brook-Shepherd, *Prelude to Infamy The Story of Chancellor Dollfuss of Austria* (Cleveland, 1962) is first rate. For an hour-by-hour account of the *Anschluss,* consult Dieter Wagner and Gerhard Tomkowitz, *Anschluss: The Week Hitler Seized Vienna* (New York, 1968). Kurt von Schuschnigg, *The Brutal Takeover* (London, 1969) is a more personal view of the *Anschluss.*

In regard to the Soviet Union, Alexsandr M. Nekrich offers a survey of German-Soviet relations between the wars in *Pariahs, Partners, Predators: German-Soviet Relations, 1922–1941* (New York, 1997). Other studies of Soviet foreign policy include Max Beloff, *The Foreign Policy of Soviet Russia 1929–1941, Vol. II, 1936–1941* (Oxford, 1949); J. Haslam, *Soviet Foreign Policy and the Struggle for Collective Security in Europe, 1933–1939* (London, 1984); Adam Ulam, *Expansion and Coexistence: The History of Soviet Foreign Policy, 1917–1967* (New York, 1968); Geoffrey Roberts, *The Unholy Alliance: Stalin's Pact with Hitler* (London, 1989) as well as his most recent book, *The Soviet Union and the Origins of the Second World War: Russo-German Relations and the Road to War, 1933–1941* (London 1995). See also Gerhard Weinburg, *Germany and the Soviet Union, 1939–1941* (Leiden, 1954); and G. Gorodotsky, editor, *Soviet Foreign Policy, 1917–1991* (London, 1994).

Polish foreign relations can be studied in Bohdan B. Budurowycz, *Polish-Soviet Relations, 1933–1939* (New York, 1963), and Josef Korbel, *Poland Between East and West: Soviet and German Diplomacy Toward Poland, 1919–1939* (Princeton, 1963). For a good survey of Polish foreign policy, there is Roman Debicki, *Foreign Policy of Poland, 1919–1939: From the Rebirth of the Polish Republic to World War II* (New York, 1962). Anna M. Cienciala, *Poland and the Western Powers, 1938–1939: A Study in the Independence of Eastern and Western Europe* (London, 1968) is essential for an understanding of Polish foreign policy. For an important revisionist interpretation of Anglo-Polish relations, see Anita Prazmowska, *Britain, Poland, and the Eastern Front, 1939* (Cambridge, U.K., 1987).

On German rearmament there is Wilhelm Diest, *The Wehrmacht and German Rearmament* (London, 1981). William Carr, *Arms, Autarky, and Aggression: German Foreign Policy, 1933–1939* (London, 1979) focuses on the relationship between politics, the economy, and military developments. Among the many books dealing with the German armed forces there are: Matthew Cooper, *The German Army, 1933–1945* (London, 1978), and *The German Air Force* (London, 1981); Edward L. Homze, *Arming the Luftwaffe; The Reich Air Ministry and the German Aircraft Industry, 1919–1939* (Lincoln, Neb., 1976); and Williamson Murray, *Luftwaffe; A History, 1933–44* (London, 1985).

The economic background to the war is covered in Bernice A. Carroll, *Design for Total War: Arms and Economics in the Third Reich* (The Hague, 1968); Alan S. Milward, *The German Economy at War* (London, 1966); Charles P. Kindleberger, *The World in Depression, 1929–1939* (Berkeley, 1973); R. J. Overy, *The Nazi Economic Recovery, 1932–1938* (London, 1982); and David E Kaiser, *Economic Diplomacy and the Origins of the Second World War* (Princeton, 1981).

John W. Wheeler-Bennett, *Munich: Prologue to Tragedy* (New York, 1948) is more than a study of the September crisis. Christopher Thorne, *The Approach to War, 1938–1939* (New York, 1967), is a useful synthesis. Donald Cameron Watt, *How War Came: The Immediate Origins of the Second World War, 1938–1939* (New York, 1989), is a thorough examination of the last two years of peace. Anthony Read and David Fisher, *The Deadly Embrace: Hitler, Stalin, and the Nazi-Soviet Pact* (New York, 1988) is a lively, dramatic narrative. Williamson Murray, *The Change in the European Balance of Power, 1938–1939: The Path to Ruin* (Princeton, 1984) is a brilliant analysis of the change in the balance of power. The role of the general staffs is discussed in *General Staffs and Diplomacy before the Second World War* (London, 1978), Adrian Preston, ed.; and *Breach of Security; The German Secret Intelligence File on Events Leading to the Second World War* (London, 1968), David Irving, ed., contains interesting material. *Knowing One's Enemies; Intelligence Assessments before the Two World Wars* edited by Ernest R. May (Princeton, 1984), should not be overlooked.

The history of Czechoslovakia can be studied in *A History of the Czechoslovak Republic, 1918–1948* (Princeton, 1973), Victor Mamatey and Radomir Luza, eds. The most recent and detailed work on the Munich Crisis is Telford Taylor, *Munich: The Price of Peace* (London, 1979). Older studies include Keith Eubank, *Munich* (Norman, 1963); Keith Robbins, *Munich, 1938* (London, 1968); and Lawrence Thomson, *The Greatest Treason: The Untold*

Story of Munich (New York, 1968). For the Sudeten-German problem, there is Radomir Luza, *The Transfer of the Sudeten Germans: A Study of Czech-German Relations, 1933–1962* (New York, 1964); and Ronald M. Smelser, *The Sudeten Problem, 1933–1939: Volkstumspolitik and the Formulation of Nazi Foreign Policy* (Middletown, Conn., 1975). Francis Loewenheim has assembled a useful collection of documents and readings on the Munich Crisis in *Peace or Appeasement? Hitler, Chamberlain, and the Munich Crisis* (Boston, 1965). For a fascinating series of on-the-spot reports from Prague consult George F. Kennan, *From Prague after Munich: Diplomatic Papers, 1938–1940* (Princeton, 1968). Jonathan Zorach, "Czechoslovakia's Fortifications: Their Development and role in the Munich Crisis," *Militargeschichtliche Mitteilungen*, 17: 2 (1976), 81–94, must not be overlooked. In *Appeasing Fascism. Articles from the Wayne State University Conference on Munich after Fifty Years* edited by Melvin Small and Otto Feinstein (Lantham, Md., 1991), see in particular, Gerald L. Weinberg, "Germany, Munich and Appeasement." Another useful collection is Maya Latynski, ed., *Reappraising the Munich Pact: Continental Perspectives* (Baltimore, 1992). On the role of Eduard Benes there is *Czechoslovakia between Stalin and Hitler: The Diplomacy of Edvard Benes in the 1930s* (Oxford, 1996) by Igor Lukes. *The Munich Crisis, 1938: Prelude to World War II,* edited by Igor Lukes and Erich Goldstein (London, 1999), is a collection of essays using new archival materials. On the aftermath of the Munich pact there is Ian R. Grimwood, *Hoping for the Best but Preparing for the Worst: The Aftermath of Munich* (London, 1998).

The best survey of British history for this period is A. J. P. Taylor, *English History, 1914–1945* (New York, 1965), perhaps Taylor's best book. There are many fine studies on aspects of British foreign policy before the war. Among these are F. S. Northedge, *The Troubled Giant: Britain Among the Great Powers, 1916–1939* (London, 1966); David Dilks, ed., *Retreat from Power; Studies in Britain's Foreign Policy in the Twentieth Century,* 2 vols., (London, 1981); C. A. MacDonald, *The United States, Britain, and Appeasement, 1936–1939* (London, 1981); Simon Newman, *March 1939: the British Guarantee to Poland* (Oxford, 1976); William R. Rock, *British Appeasement in the 1930s* (London, 1977); Sidney Aster, *1939: The Making of the Second World War* (London, 1973);

and Keith Middlemas, *Diplomacy of Illusion: The British Government and Germany, 1937–1939* (London, 1972); Correlli Barnett, *The Collapse of British Power* (London, 1972); Franklin R. Gannon, *The British Press and Germany, 1936–1939* (Oxford, 1971); David Carlton, *MacDonald versus Henderson; The Foreign Policy of the Second Labor Government* (London, 1970). For the Anglo-German Naval Treaty there is Eva H. Haraszti, *Treaty-breakers or Realpolitiker? The Anglo-German Naval Agreement of June 1935* (Boppard am Rhein, Germany, 1973).

The problem of appeasement can be studied in Keith Robbins, *Appeasement*, 2nd ed., (Oxford, 1997); Martin Gilbert and Richard Gott, *The Appeasers* (Boston, 1963); Margaret George, *The Warped Vision: British Foreign Policy, 1933–1939* (Pittsburgh, 1965); Martin Gilbert, *The Roots of Appeasement* (London, 1966), which places the subject in historical perspective; Ritchie Ovendale, *Appeasement and the English-Speaking World* (Cardiff, 1975); Larry W. Fuchser, *Neville Chamberlain: A Study in the Politics of History* (New York, 1982); Neville Thompson, *The Anti-Appeasers: Conservative Opposition to Appeasement* (Oxford, 1971); D. C. Watt, *Personalities and Politics: Studies in the Formation of British Foreign Policy and its Critics, 1938–1939* (Notre Dame, 1965). On the relationship of the British economy and financial system to foreign policy, consult G. C. Peden, *British Rearmament and the Treasury, 1932–1939* (Edinburgh, 1979) and Robert Paul Shay, *British Rearmament in the Thirties: Politics and Profits* (London, 1977). Richard Cockett, *Twilight of Truth: Chamberlain, Appeasement and the Manipulation of the Press* (New York, 1989) studies the role of the press and the politics of appeasement, 1937–1940. Frank McDonough examines appeasement in the British government, society and in the political parties in *Neville Chamberlain, Appeasement and the British Road to War* (Manchester, U.K., 1998). For an analysis of British naval diplomacy towards Germany, read Joseph A. Maiola, *The Royal Navy and Nazi Germany, 1933–1939: A Study in Appeasement and the Origins of the Second World War* (London, 1998). Paul W. Doer surveys British foreign policy in *British Foreign Policy, 1919–1939 'Hope for the Best, Prepare for the Worst'* (Manchester, U.K., 1998). Britain's Mediterranean strategy is the subject of Lawrence R. Pratt's important book, *East of Malta, West of Suez: Britain's Mediterranean Crisis, 1936–1939* (Cambridge,

U.K., 1975). Chamber-lain's appeasement policy is detailed in R. A. C. Parker, *Chamberlain and Appeasement. British Policy and the Coming of the Second World War* (New York, 1993). For the attitude of the British weekly press with regard to Nazi Germany, there is Benny Morris, *The Roots of Appeasement: The British Weekly Press and Nazi Germany During the 1930s* (London, 1991).

Among the books which examine British military and naval policies are Uri Bialer, *The Shadow of the Bomber: Fear of Air Attack and British Politics, 1932–1939* (London, 1980); P. J. Dennis, *Decision by Default: Peacetime Conscription and British Defence, 1919–1939* (London, 1972); F. H. Hinsley, et al., *British Intelligence in the Second World War*, Vol. I (London, 1979); Michael Howard, *The Continental Commitment: The Dilemma of British Defence Policy in the Era of the Two World Wars* (London, 1972); Brian Bond, *British Military Policy between the Two World Wars* (Oxford, 1989); N. H. Gibbs, *Rearmament Policy* (London, 1976), Volume I in J. R. M. Butler, ed., *Grand Strategy*, in the military series of the British Official History of the Second World War; H. Montgomery Hyde, *British Air Policy Between the Wars, 1918–1939* (London, 1976); Stephen Roskill, *Naval Policy Between the Wars*, 2 vols. (London, 1976, 1986); Malcolm S. Smith, *British Air Strategy Between the Wars* (Oxford, 1984). Christopher Andrew, *Her Majesty's Secret Service The Making of the British Intelligence Community* (New York, 1986); Wesley K. Wark, *The Ultimate Enemy: British Intelligence and Nazi Germany, 1933–1939* (Ithaca, 1985) deal with the weaknesses of British military intelligence. Gaines Post, Jr., *Dilemmas of Appeasement: British Deterrence and Defense, 1934–1937* (Ithaca, 1993)

Among the books on American foreign policy there is William Langer and S. Everett Gleason, *The Challenge to Isolationism, 1937–1939* (New York, 1952). For foreign policy on the presidential level, see Robert A. Dallek, *Franklin D. Roosevelt and American Foreign Policy, 1932–1945* (New York, 1979), and on the United States and Nazi Germany consult Arnold A. Offner, *American Appeasement: United States Foreign Policy and Germany, 1933–1938* (Cambridge, Mass., 1969). The Anglo-American relationship is discussed by Callum A. MacDonald, *The United States, Britain, and Appeasement, 1936–1939* (New York, 1981); James R. Leutze, *Bargaining for Supremacy: Anglo-American Naval Collabo-*

ration, 1937–1941 (Chapel Hill, 1977); and David Reynolds, *The Creation of the Anglo-American Alliance, 1937–1941* (New York, 1981). An examination of British establishment policy towards France can be found in Michael Dockrill, *British Establishment Perspectives on France, 1936–1940* (London, 1999).

On France, Alexander Werth, *The Twilight of France, 1933–1940,* I (New York, 1942) can still be read with profit. Anthony P. Adamthwaite, *France and the Coming of the Second World War, 1936–1939* (London, 1977) is a major work, based on archival materials. His book, *Grandeur and Misery: France's Bid for Power in Europe, 1914–1940* (New York, 1995), is a brilliant survey of French foreign policy. Joel Colton, *Leon Blum: Humanist in Politics* (New York, 1966), is the definitive biography. Geoffrey Warner, *Pierre Laval and the Eclipse of France, 1931–1945* (New York, 1968), is a good biography although the author was unable to use French documents. The only treatment of the Franco-Soviet Pact is William Evan Scott, *Alliance Against Hitler: The Origins of the Franco-Soviet Pact* (Durham, N.C., 1962). On the relation of military policy and foreign policy, read Robert J. Young, *In Command of France: French Foreign Policy and Military Planning: 1933–1940* (Cambridge, Mass., 1978), and also his book, *France and the Origins of the Second World War* (New York, 1996). French foreign policy is examined in three fine books: Stephen A. Schuker, *The End of French Predominance in Europe* (Chapel Hill, 1976); Marc Trachtenburg, *Reparations in World Politics: France and European Economic Diplomacy, 1916–1923* (New York, 1980); and Walter A. McDougall, *France's Rhineland Diplomacy 1914–1924: The Last Bid for Power in Europe* (Princeton, 1978). Anglo-French appeasement policies are studied in Thomas Martin, *Britain, France und Appeasement: Anglo-French relations in the Popular Front Era* (London, 1996); and Richard Davis, *Anglo-French Relations before the Second World War: Appeasement and Crisis* (London, 2001).

Among the memoirs and biographies of British political leaders and generals, Winston S. Churchill, *The Gathering Storm* (Boston, 1948) is a classic, but had Churchill been a member of the Baldwin and Chamberlain governments and thus responsible for war or peace, he would have written an entirely different book. There is the official biography, Martin Gilbert, *Winston S. Churchill, 1922–1939: The Prophet of Truth,* vol. 5, (Boston,

1977), filled with useful information. William Manchester, *The Last Lion: Winston Spencer Churchill: Alone 1932–1940* (Boston, 1988), is dramatic and colorful. *The Memoirs of Anthony Eden, The Earl of Avon: Facing the Dictators* (Boston, 1962) reveal more than Eden realized about his attitude concerning appeasement. For a critical biography of Eden there is David Carlton, *Anthony Eden* (London, 1981). R. J. Minney, *Private Papers of Hore-Belisha* (London, 1960); and Alfred Duff Cooper, *Old Men Forget* (London 1953), contain accounts of discussions in the Chamberlain cabinet. Two very important sources on British foreign policy are David Dilks, ed., *The Diaries of Sir Alexander Cadogan, 1938–1945* (New York, 1972); and Oliver Harvey, *The Diplomatic Diaries of Oliver Harvey, 1937–1949* (London, 1970). Keith Feiling, *The Life of Neville Chamberlain* (London 1946), and Iain Macleod, *Neville Chamberlain* (London 1961), are sympathetic studies useful for quotations from his letters and diaries. John Charmley, *Chamberlain and the Lost Peace* (London, 1989), is a revisionist view of Chamberlain. A more critical opinion is presented by Frank McDonough, *Neville Chamberlain and the British Road to War* (Manchester, U.K., 1998). Chamberlain's failures in rearming Britain are the subject of John Ruggiero's excellent study, *Neville Chamberlain and British Rearmament: Pride, Prejudice, and Politics* (Westport, Conn., 1993). For Stanley Baldwin there is Keith Middlemas and John Barnes, *Baldwin: A Biography* (London, 1969). Andrew Roberts has written a sympathetic biography of Halifax, *'The Holy Fox,' A Biography of Lord Halifax* (London, 1991). Ian Colvin, *None So Blind: A British View of the Origins of World War II* (New York, 1965) is useful chiefly for the quotations from the papers of Lord Vansittart. Appeasement is defended in Samuel Hoare, *Viscount Templewood, Nine Troubled Years* (London, 1954), and in Neville Henderson, *Failure of a Mission: Berlin, 1937–1939* (New York,1940). See also Peter Nevelle, *Appeasing Hitler: The Diplomacy of Sir Neville Henderson,* (London, 2000). Lord Strang, *At Home and Abroad* (London 1956) throws light on the Czechoslovak crisis and the Moscow talks in the summer of 1939. Ivone Kirkpatrick, *The Inner Circle* (London, 1959) describes British diplomacy in Berlin. Military problems are covered in *Time Unguarded: The Ironside Diaries, 1937–1940,* edited by Roderick Macleod and Denis Kelly (New York, 1962);

The Liddell Hart Memoirs, 2 vols. (New York, 1965–1966); Sir John Slessor, *The Central Blue: Recollections and Reflections* (London,1956); *Chief of Staff: The Diaries of Lieutenant-General Sir Henry Pownall,* Brian Bond, ed., vol. I, 1933–1940 (Hampden, Conn.). The perspective from the Labor benches can be found in Hugh Dalton, *The Fateful Years: Memories, 1931–1945* (London, 1957), and *Harold Nicolson, Diaries and Letters, 1930–1939* (New York, 1966).

Among German memoirs and biographies, Henry A. Turner, *Stresemann and the Politics of the Weimar Republic* (Princeton, 1963) is important, as well as Hans Gatzke, *Stresemann and the Rearmament of Germany* (Baltimore, 1954). For Schacht, the Nazi minister of economy, see Amos E. Simpson, *Hjalmar Schacht in Perspective* (The Hague, 1969). *The Von Hassell Diaries, 1938–44* (London, 1948) tell the story of a diplomat who opposed Hitler and paid for it with his life.

Eduard Benes wrote a survey of the Munich crisis, *Memoirs From Munich to New War and Victory* (Boston, 1954); it is not significant. His more detailed account of the Munich Crisis has never been translated into English, but there is an excellent summary in Otakar Odlozilik, "Eduard Benes on Munich Days," *Journal of Central European Affairs,* IX (January, 1950): 419–428.

For the Polish side there are *Papers and Memoirs of Jozef Lipski, Ambassador of Poland: Diplomat in Berlin, 1933–1939,* edited by Waclaw Jedrzejewicz (New York, 1958); and his *Diplomat in Paris, 1936–1939: Papers and Memoirs of Juliusz Łukasiewicz, Ambassador of Poland,* (New York, 1970).

On Italian foreign policy, read *Ciano's Diary, 1937–1938* (New York, 1953); *The Ciano Diaries, 1939–1943* (New York, 1946), and *Ciano's Diplomatic Papers* (London, 1948).

Among the older documentary collections, *Trials of the Major War Criminals before the International Military Tribunal, Proceedings and Documents,* 43 vols. (Nuremberg, 1947–49) is still unique. Many of the documents collected for the trial have been published in *Nazi Conspiracy and Aggression,* 10 vols. (Washington, D.C., 1946–48). There is some useful material on German foreign policy in the trials of the minor war criminals, *Trials of the War Criminals before the Nuremberg Military Tribunals under Control Council Law N. 10* (Washington, D.C., n.d.). The archives of the

German foreign ministry captured in the closing days of the war have been published jointly by the British, American, and French governments in *Documents on German Foreign Policy, 1918–1945, from the Archives of the German Foreign Ministry*, Series C, 1933–1937, 7 vols. (Washington, D.C.,1957–83), Series D, 1938–1939, 7 vols., (Washington, D.C., 1949–1956). Because of the cost of publishing so large a collection, only documents for the period 1933–45 appear in English. Documents for the years 1925–33 have appeared in the series, *Akten zur Deutschen Auswärtigen Politik 1918–1945, aus dem Archiv des Auswärtigen Amt* (Göttingen, Germany, 1966–). Documents on Soviet-German relations are available in *Nazi-Soviet Relations, 1939–1944: Documents from the Archives of the German Foreign Office* (Washington, D.C., 1948). The Soviet government published German documents dealing with Anglo-German affairs in *Documents and Materials relating to the Eve of the Second World War*, 2 vols. (Moscow, 1948); the second volume includes private papers of Herbert von Dirksen.

The British government has published *Documents on British Foreign Policy 1919–1939;* 2nd series 1929–1938, 21 vols.; and 3rd series, 1938–1939, 9 vols. (London 1946–55). The British archives, housed in the Public Record Office, Kew, are opened to the public.

French diplomatic documents had been published in *Documents Diplomatiques Français*, Série I, 1932–1935, 13 vols. (Paris, 1964–1984); and Série 2, 1936–1939 (Paris, 1963–1986). The record of the parliamentary investigation of the origins of the war and the defeat of France has been published in *Les événements survenus en France de 1933 à 1945. Temoignages et documents recueillis par la commission d'enquete parlementaire*, 11 vols. (Paris, 1947–51).

Foreign Relations of the United States: Diplomatic Papers, published annually, is available for the entire post–1919 period. In addition, as part of this series, The United States government has published 13 volumes on the Paris Peace Conference of 1919—the only major power to do so.

The Italian government has published a voluminous collection of source materials covering Italian foreign policy since 1861, *I Documenti Diplomatici Italiani* (Rome, 1952) in nine series. Series six, seven, and eight are pertinent to the study of the origins of World War II. Belgian documents are available in *Documents diplomatiques belges, 1920–1940,* vols. 4 and 5, *La politique de sécurité extérieure, 1936–1940* (Brussels, 1965–1966).

The only Polish documents are in a Polish White Book published at the outbreak of the war: *Official Documents Concerning Polish-German and Polish-Soviet Relations, 1933–1939* (New York, 1940). Czechoslovak documents can be found in *Germany and Czechoslovakia, 1918–1945: Documents on German Policies,* edited by Koloman Gajan and Robert Kvacek (Prague, 1965); *Das Abkommen von Munchen 1938: Tschechoslovakische diplomatische Dokumente, 1937–1939,* edited by Vaclav Kral (Prague, 1968); *Die Deutschen in der Tschechoslowakei, 1933–1947,* edited by Vaclav Kral (Prague, 1964) and *New Documents on the History of Munich* (Prague, 1958). *Soviet Efforts on the Eve of World War II* (September 1938–August, 1939), 2 vols. (Moscow, 1973) contains some revealing documents on Soviet negotiations. *Soviet Documents on Foreign Policy,* edited by Jane Degras, 3 vols., (London, 1951–53), contains public speeches and Soviet diplomatic correspondence which have been published in other collections.

Specialized studies on topics in prewar diplomacy appear in *Journal of Modern History, Journal of Contemporary History, Vierteljahrshefte für Zeitgeschichte, Revue de l'histoire de la Deuxième Guerre Mondiale, Historical Journal, International History Review, Journal of Strategic Studies, Journal of Strategic Studies, History, International History Review, Slavic Review, English Historical Review, Diplomacy and Statecraft,* and *International Affairs* (Moscow).

INDEX

The Origins of World War II, Third Edition
Developmental editor: Andrew J. Davidson
Editor/production editor: Lucy Herz
Printer: McNaughton & Gunn, Inc.